Latin

for
Roman Catholics

Answer Key

Thomas K. Capps

©Thomas K. Capps, 2019

Forward

This book is a supplement and answer key to the second edition (2019) of *Latin for Roman Catholics* by Thomas Capps. The purpose of this supplement is twofold. First, it is intended as an aid to teachers who might need guidance on a particular Latin *sententia* or two. Some of the *sententiae* in *Latin for Roman Catholics* are difficult or obscure, and it is helpful to see an explanation for their translations before attempting to teach them. The second intended use of this answer key is for the students themselves. Seeing the correct translation explained can be invaluable even if the student has an instructor to explain it well. Provided one has first wrestled with the Latin *sententia,* reading the translation in the answer key can enhance learning.

To serve these two goals, the translations given in this answer key are exceptionally literal. As much as possible, the Latin words are translated individually into English in their most basic grammatical meaning. This makes the grammar and vocabulary of each *sententia* abundantly clear. The sacrifice of such an approach, of course, is that the translations are often in very poor English. Students and teachers therefore should use these translations exclusively as an aid to untangling the Latin; in general, students should not submit a copy of these translations as their own, and teachers should not accept them.

Yet, where the extreme literalism results in truly incoherent English, explanations of the meaning are given in parentheses. For example, the translation for number twenty-eight of chapter six reads: *He stands with (in) the shadow of a great name.* The literal grammar gives *with* but the English requires *in*. However, such explanations have been avoided as much as possible.

Where English absolutely requires the addition of a word which is implied but not present in the Latin, that word is placed in brackets. For example, the translation for number seventeen of chapter nine reads: *Either I will find a way or I will make [one]*. 'One' is not present in the Latin because Latin grammar does not require it; English grammar, however, necessitates it.

It must also be noted that although extreme literalism has been attempted, Latin words may not always be translated exactly the same throughout the book. An attempt has been made to avoid such variation, yet in the end it could not be completely avoided.

God bless you, *et feliciter legatis!*

Sententiae

Chapter Two

1. Aurora Musis amica. (Erasmus)
   Dawn is a friend to the Muses.

2. Fortuna est caeca. (Cicero)
   Fortune is blind.

3. Fama volat. (Virgil)
   Fame flies.

4. Fata obstant. (Virgil)
   The Fates stand in the way.

5. Ave Maria gratia plena (episcopal motto)
   Hail Mary, full with grace

6. State (episcopal motto)
   Stand!

7. Video et taceo (motto of Elizabeth I of England)
   I see and I refrain from speaking.

8. Sapientia et doctrina (motto of Fordham University)
   Wisdom and doctrine

9. Pro gloria et patria (motto of Prussia)
   For glory and homeland

10. Dum spiro spero (motto of South Carolina)
    While I breathe, I hope.

11. Ad Jesum per Mariam (Catholic phrase)
    Towards Jesus through Mary

12. Nihil obstat (printed on Catholic books)
    Nothing stands in the way.

13. Habemus papam (said at the announcement of a new pope)
    We have a pope!

14. Nihil nimis (Latin proverb)
    Nothing excessively

Chapter Three

1. Dominus protector vitae meae. (Ps.26:1)
   The Lord is the protector of my life.

2. Quis sicut Dominus Deus noster? (Ps.112:5)
   Who is like the Lord our God?

3. Dominus dat sapientiam. (Prv.2:6)
   The Lord gives wisdom.

4. Sicut lilium inter spinas, sic amica mea inter filias. (SS.2:2)
   Like a lily among thorns, just so is my girlfriend among daughters.

5. Deo gratias (at Mass)
   Thanks be to God.

6. Gloria tibi Domine (at Mass)
   Glory to you, Lord!

7. Non Angli, sed angeli! (Gregory the Great)
   Not Englishmen, but angels!

8. Servus servorum Dei (Gregory the Great, title of Pope)
   Servant of the servants of God

9. Historia… vitae magistra. (Cicero)
   History is the teacher of life.

10. Ora et labora (Benedictine motto)
    Pray and work!

11. Ad Gloriam Dei (episcopal motto)
    Towards the glory of God

12. Amo te Domine (episcopal motto)
    I love you, Lord.

13. Christus vita nostra (episcopal motto)
    Christ is our life.

14. Deus et patria (episcopal motto)
    God and homeland

15. Domini nostri Jesu Christi (episcopal motto)
    Of our Lord Jesus Christ

16. Dominus est (episcopal motto)
    It is the Lord!

17. In Deo spero (episcopal motto)
    In God I hope.

18. Magnus Deus noster (episcopal motto)
    Great is our God.

19. Propter te Domine (episcopal motto)
    Because of you, Lord.

20. Regnat Christus Dominus (episcopal motto)
    Christ the Lord reigns.

21. Regnat Deus (episcopal motto)
    God reigns.

22. State in Domino (episcopal motto)
    Stand in the Lord!

23. Sub umbra Carmeli (episcopal motto)
    Under the shadow of Carmel

24. Sub umbra Petri (episcopal motto)
    Under the shadow of Peter

25. Vigilate et orate (episcopal motto)
    Keep vigil and pray!

26. Regnat populus (motto of Arkansas)
    The people reign.

27. In Deo speramus (motto of Brown University)
    In God we hope.

28. Gloriosus et liber (motto of Manitoba)
    Glorious and free

29. Nihil sine Deo (motto of Romania)
    Nothing without God

30. Semper liber (motto of Victoria, BC)
    Always free

31. Sic semper tyrannis (motto of Virginia)
    Thus always to tyrants

32. Ora pro nobis (Catholic phrase)
    Pray for us

33. Exempli gratia (commonly abbreviated as *e.g.*)
    Grace of an example

34. In te speramus, ad te clamamus: ora, ora pro nobis. (*O Sanctissima*)
    In you we hope, towards you we call: pray, pray for us.

Chapter Four

1. Laudate Dominum de caelis, laudate eum in excelsis. (Ps.148:1)
   Praise the Lord down from the heavens, praise him in the highests.

2. Deus enim in caelo, et tu super terram. (Ecc.5:1)
   For God is in heaven, and you are on the earth.

3. Dignum et justum est. (at Mass)
   It is worthy and just.

4. Sanctus, Sanctus, Sanctus Dominus Deus Sabaoth. Pleni sunt caeli et terra gloria tua. Hosanna in excelsis. (at Mass)
   Holy, holy, holy Lord God of Hosts. The heavens and the earth are full with your glory. Hosanna in the highests.

5. Agnus Dei, qui tollis peccata mundi, miserere nobis. Agnus Dei, qui tollis peccata mundi, miserere nobis. Agnus Dei, qui tollis peccata mundi, dona nobis pacem. (at Mass)
   Lamb of God, you who take away the sins of the world, have mercy on us. Lamb of God, you who take away the sins of the world, have mercy on us. Lamb of God, you who take away the sins of the world, grant to us peace.

6. Valde magnum est in obedientia stare. (a Kempis)
   It is very great to stand in obedience.

7. Est deus in nobis. (Ovid)
   There is god in us.

8. Auxilium meum a Domino (episcopal motto)
   My help is from the Lord.

9. Dominus Deus magnus est (episcopal motto)
   The Lord God is great.

10. Evangelii servus (episcopal motto)
    Servant of the Gospel

11. Evangelium Dei evangelizare (episcopal motto)
    To preach the Gospel of God

12. In auxilium meum festina Domine (episcopal motto)
    O Lord, hurry into my help!

13. Per arma Christi (episcopal motto)
    Through the weapons of Christ

14. Pro regno Dei (episcopal motto)
    For the kingdom of God

15. Propter Jesum et evangelium (episcopal motto)
    Because of Jesus and the Gospel

16. Propter regnum Dei (episcopal motto)
    Because of the kingdom of God

17. Regnum tuum Domine (episcopal motto)
    Your kingdom, Lord!

18. Festina lente (motto of Augustus)
    Hurry slowly.

19. Domina nostra, auxilium Christianorum (title of Mary)
    Our Lady, help of Christians

20. Evangelium vitae (encyclical of John Paul the Great)
    The Gospel of Life

21. Ave Maria, gratia plena, Dominus tecum. Benedicta tu in mulieribus, et benedictus fructus ventris tui Jesus. Sancta Maria, Mater Dei, ora pro nobis peccatoribus, nunc et in hora mortis nostrae. Amen. (Catholic Prayer)
Hail Mary, full with grace, the Lord is with you. Blessed are you among women, and blessed is the fruit of your womb, Jesus. Holy Mary, Mother of God, pray for us, sinners, now and in the hour of our death. Amen.

Chapter Five

1. In Deo laudabo verbum, in Domino laudabo… (Ps.55:10)
I will praise the word in God, in the Lord I will praise!

2. Misericordias Domini in aeternum cantabo. (Ps.88:1)
I will sing the mercies of the Lord into eternity.

3. Beatus vir qui timet Dominum: in mandatis ejus volet nimis. (Ps.111:1)
Blessed is the man who fears the Lord: in his commands he delights excessively.

4. Laudate Dominum, quia bonus Dominus. (Ps.134:3)
Praise the Lord, because the Lord is good.

5. Deus, canticum novum cantabo tibi. (Ps.143:9)
God, I will sing a new canticle to you.

6. Lauda, anima mea, Dominum. Laudabo Dominum in vita mea. (Ps.145:2)
My soul, praise the Lord! I will praise the Lord in my life.

7. Regnabit Dominus in saecula. (Ps.145:10)
The Lord will reign into the ages.

8. Videbitis, et gaudebit cor vestrum. (Isa.66:14)
Y'all will see, and your heart will rejoice.

9. … in Domino gaudebo, et exsultabo in Deo Jesu meo. (Hab.3:18)
I will rejoice in the Lord, and I will exalt in God my Jesus.

10. Dominus Deus tuus… gaudebit super te… exsultabit super te. (Zeph.3:17)
The Lord your God will rejoice over you, will exalt over you.

11. Gratias tibi, bone Jesu, pastor aeterne. (a Kempis)
Thanks to you, good Jesus, eternal shepherd.

12. Multa verba non satiant animam, sed bona vita refrigerat mentem, et pura conscientia magnam ad Deum praestat confidentiam. (a Kempis)
    Many words do not satisfy the soul, but a good life cools the mind and a pure conscience bestows great confidence towards God.

13. Periculum in mora. (Livy)
    There is danger in delay.

14. Arma non servant modum. (Seneca)
    Weapons do not preserve moderation.

15. Modum tenere debemus. (Seneca)
    We ought to hold moderation.

16. Novum Testamentum (Catholic phrase)
    The New Testament

Chapter Six

1. Honora patrem tuum et matrem. (Dt.5:16)
   Honor your father and mother.

2. Initium sapientiae timor Domini. (Ps.110:10, Sir.1:16)
   The beginning of wisdom is the fear of the Lord.

3. Laudate, pueri, Dominum, laudate nomen Domini. (Ps.112:1)
   Boys, praise the Lord, praise the name of the Lord!

4. Veritas Domini manet in aeternum. (Ps.116:2)
   The truth of the Lord remains into eternity.

5. Magnus Dominus noster, et magna virtus ejus, et sapientiae ejus non est numerus. (Ps.146:5)
   Great is our Lord, and great is his virtue, and of his wisdom there is not a number.

6. Nihil sub sole novum. (Ecc.1:10)
   Nothing under the sun is new.

7. Timor Domini gloria. (Sir.1:11)
   The fear of the Lord is glory.

8. Sapientia enim et disciplina timor Domini. (Sir.1:34)
   For wisdom and discipline are fear of the Lord.

9. Qui timet Dominum honorat parentes. (Sir.3:8)
   He who fears the Lord honors the parents.

10. In opere et sermone… honora patrem tuum. (Sir.3:9)
    In deed and speech honor your father.

11. Ecce homo! (Jn.19:5)
    Behold the human!

12. Deus caritas est. (1Jn.4:8)
    God is love.

13. Timor non est in caritate. (1Jn.4:18)
    Fear is not in love.

14. Laus tibi Christe (at Mass)
    Praise to you, Christ.

15. Sursum corda. Habemus ad Dominum. (at Mass)
    Upwards hearts! We have towards the Lord.

16. Laus tibi, Domine, Rex aeternae gloriae (said in the Divine Office during Lent in place of the Alleluia)
    Praise to you, Lord, king of eternal glory.

17. Ecce lignum crucis. (Good Friday Antiphon)
    Behold the wood of the Cross!

18. Christus Rex (Liturgical feast)
    Christ the King

19. Sacramentum caritatis (Aquinas about the Mass)
    The Sacrament of Love

20. De Civitate Dei (title of Augustine's masterpiece)
    About the City of God

21. In voluntate ejus pax nostra. (Dante)
    In his will is our peace.

22. In regione caecorum rex est luscus. (Erasmus)
    In the region of the blind, the one-eyed man is king.

23. Gratias tibi, bone Jesu, lux lucis aeternae. (a Kempis)
    Thanks to you, good Jesus, light of eternal light.

24. Leges habent perquam paucas. (Thomas More describing Utopia)
    They have extremely few laws.

25. O tempora! O mores! (Cicero)
    O the times! O the customs!

26. Silent enim leges inter arma. (Cicero)
    For laws are silent among weapons.

27. Leges sine moribus vanae. (Horace)
    Laws without customs are vain.

28. Stat magni nominis umbra. (Lucan about Pompey)
    He stands with (in) the shadow of a great name.

29. Non est princeps super leges, sed leges supra principem. (Pliny)
    A prince is not above the laws, but the laws are over the prince.

30. A Cruce victoria (episcopal motto)
    From the Cross is victory

31. Ad Deum pro hominibus (episcopal motto)
    Towards God for humans

32. Ad gloriam Dei et pacem in terris (episcopal motto)
    Towards the glory of God and peace in the lands

33. Ad lucem per Crucem (episcopal motto)
    Towards light through the Cross

34. Amor Crucis armis lucis (episcopal motto)
    Love of the Cross with weapons of light

35. Amore amoris tui (episcopal motto)
    With the love of your love

36. Amore non timore (episcopal motto)
    With love, not with fear

37. Caritas in veritate (episcopal motto)
    Charity in truth

38. Caritate veritatis (episcopal motto)
    With the charity of the truth

39. Christus pax nostra (episcopal motto)
    Christ is our peace.

40. Gloria Deo pax hominibus (episcopal motto)
    Glory to God, peace to humans

41. Sub lumine Matris (episcopal motto)
    Under the light of the Mother

42. Sub Mariae nomine (episcopal motto)
    Under the name of Mary

43. Non nobis, Domine, non nobis, sed nomine tuo da gloriam. (Ps.113:9, motto of the Knights Templar)
    Not with us, Lord, not with us, but with your name give the glory.

44. Virtute et armis (motto of Mississippi)
    With virtue and weapons

45. In Christi lumine pro mundi vita (motto of the Pontifical Catholic University of Chile)
    In the light of Christ for the life of the world

46. Via Crucis (Catholic devotion)
    The Way of the Cross

47. Opus Dei (Religious Organization)
    Work of God

48. Cor Jesu… inflamma cor nostrum amore tui. (Sacred Heart Novena)
    Heart of Jesus, inflame our heart with love of you.

49. …angelum pacis: Michael (*Christe Sanctorum*)
    … the angel of peace: Michael

12. Sanctifica eos in veritate. Sermo tuus veritas est. (Jn.17:17)
    Sanctify them in truth. Your speech is truth.

13. Dominus autem Spiritus est: ubi autem Spiritus Domini, ibi libertas. (2Cor.3:17)
    The Lord, however, is Spirit: where, however, the Spirit of the Lord is, there is liberty.

14. Ubi caritas et amor, Deus ibi est. (Holy Thursday Antiphon)
    Where there is charity and love, God is there.

15. Causa finalis est causa causarum. (Aquinas)
    The final cause is the cause of causes.

16. Finis legis non est lex. (Aquinas)
    The end of law is not the law.

17. Ubi amor, ibi oculus. (Aquinas)
    Where there is love, there is an eye (i.e. clear thinking).

18. Ultima hominis felicitas est in contemplatione veritatis. (Aquinas)
    The ultimate happiness of a human is in the contemplation of truth.

19. Caritas radix est omnium operum bonorum. (Augustine)
    Charity is the root of all good deeds.

20. In necessitatibus, unitas; in diversis, libertas; sed in omnibus, caritas. (Augustine)
    In necessities, unity; in diversities, freedom; but in all things, charity.

21. Magnus es, domine, et laudabilis valde. (beginning of Augustine's *Confessions*)
    You are great, O Lord, and very laudable.

22. Simul justus et peccator. (Augustine)
    At the same time just and a sinner.

23. Historia vero testis temporum, lux veritatis, vita memoriae, magistra vitae, nuntia vetustatis. (Cicero)
    History is truly the witness of the times, the light of truth, the life of memory, the teacher of life, the messenger of old age.

24. Mater omnium bonarum artium sapientia est. (Cicero)
    The mother of all good arts is wisdom.

25. Philosophia est ars vitae. (Cicero)
    Philosophy is the art of life.

50. Laus, honor, virtus, gloria, Deo Patri et Filio, Sancto simul Paraclito, in saeculorum saecula. (Ambrose, *Jesu Corona Virginum*)
    Praise, honor, virtue, glory to God the Father and the Son and, at the same time, the Holy Paraclete, into the ages of ages.

Chapter Seven

1. Dominus excelsus, terribilis, rex magnus super omnem terram. (Ps.46:3)
    The highest Lord, terrible, great king over all the earth.

2. Rex omnis terrae Deus. (Ps.46:8)
    God is king of all the earth.

3. Magnus Dominus et laudabilis nimis, in civitate Dei nostri, in monte sancto ejus. (Ps.47:2)
    Great is the Lord and excessively laudable in the city of our God, on his holy mountain.

4. Misericordias Domini in aeternum cantabo: in generationem et generationem, annuntiabo veritatem tuam in ore meo. (Ps.88:1)
    The mercies of the Lord I will sing into eternity: into generation and generation I will announce your truth in my mouth.

5. Excelsus super omnes gentes Dominus, et super caelos gloria ejus. (Ps.112:4)
    Highest over all the nations is the Lord, and over the heavens is his glory.

6. Laudate omnes gentes, laudate Dominum. (Ps.117:1)
    All nations, praise, praise the Lord!

7. Beati omnes qui timent Dominum, qui ambulant in viis ejus. (Ps.127:1)
    Blessed are all who fear the Lord, who walk in his ways.

8. Omnia flumina intrant in mare. (Ecc.1:7)
    All rivers enter into the sea.

9. Radix sapientiae est timere Dominum. (Sir.1:25)
    The root of wisdom is to fear the Lord.

10. Et ambulabunt gentes in lumine tuo, et reges in splendore ortus tui. (Isa.60:3)
    And nations will walk in your light, and kings in the splendor of your rising.

11. Beati pauperes, quia vestrum est regnum Dei. (Lk.6:20)
    Blessed are the poor, because yours is the kingdom of God.

26. Ars longa, vita brevis. (Hippocrates)
    Art is long, life is short.

27. Est natura hominum novitatis avida. (Pliny the Elder)
    The nature of humans is desirous of newness.

28. Omnis ars naturae imitatio est. (Seneca)
    Every art is imitation of nature.

29. Rationale enim animal est homo. (Seneca)
    For a human is a rational animal.

30. Auribus teneo lupum. (Terence)
    I hold the wolf with (by) the ears.

31. Fortes fortuna adjuvat. (Terence)
    Fortune helps the strong.

32. A Deo omnia (episcopal motto)
    From God are all things.

33. Amore et fortitudine (episcopal motto)
    With love and fortitude

34. Christus omnia in omnibus (episcopal motto)
    Christ is all things in all things.

35. Fortitudo mea Deus (episcopal motto)
    My strength is God.

36. Testimonium de lumine (episcopal motto)
    Witness about light

37. Testimonium veritati (episcopal motto)
    Witness of the truth

38. A mari usque ad mare (motto of Canada)
    From sea all the way to sea

39. Justitia omnibus (motto of D.C.)
    Justice to all

40. Veritas, bonitas, pulchritudo, sanctitas (motto of Fu Jen Catholic University)
    Truth, goodness, beauty, sanctity

41. Scientia et sapientia (motto of Illinois Wesleyan University)
    Science and wisdom

42. Ex amicitia pax (motto of international diplomacy)
    Out of friendship, peace

43. Lumen Gentium (Vatican II document)
    Light of the Nations

44. Felix qui nihil debet. (Latin Proverb)
    Happy is he who owes nothing.

45. Non omnis qui nobis arridet amicus est. (Latin Proverb)
    Not everyone who smiles towards to us is a friend.

46. Omne initium difficile. (Latin Proverb)
    Every beginning is difficult.

47. Sanctus Deus, Sanctus Fortis, Sanctus Immortalis, miserere nobis et totius mundi. (Divine Mercy Chaplet)
    Holy God, Holy Mighty One, Holy Immortal One, have mercy on us and on the whole world.

48. Christe sol justitiae (Ambrose, *Jam Christe Sol Justitiae*)
    O Christ, sun of justice!

49. Jesu, decus angelicum, in aure dulce canticum, in ore mel mirificum, in corde nectar caelicum. (Bernard, *Jesu Dulcis Memoria*)
    O Jesus, angelic honor, sweet canticle in the ear, marvel-making honey in the mouth, heavenly nectar in the heart!

50. Angelus fortis: Gabriel (*Christe Sanctorum*)
    The strong angel: Gabriel

51. Jesu clemens pie Deus, Jesu dulcis amor meus, Jesu bone, Jesu pie, Fili Dei et Mariae. (*De Amore Jesu*)
    O Jesus, clement, pious God; O Jesus, my sweet love; O good Jesus, O pious Jesus, O Son of God and Mary!

52. Jesu, nostra… jubilatio cordis, oris, et aurium. (*Jesu Nostra Refectio*)
    O Jesus, our jubilation of heart, mouth, and ears!

53. Te splendor et virtus Patris, te vita, Jesu, cordium… laudamus inter Angelos. (Urban VIII, *Te Splendor et Virtus Patris*)
    Among the angels we praise you, O Jesus, splendor and virtue of the Father, life of hearts.

54. Confiteor Deo omnipotenti, beatae Mariae semper Virgini, beato Michaeli Archangelo, beato Joanni Baptistae, sanctis Apostolis Petro et Paulo, omnibus Sanctis, et tibi, pater, quia peccavi nimis cogitatione, verbo et opere, mea culpa, mea culpa, mea maxima culpa. Ideo precor beatam Mariam semper Virginem, beatum Michaelem Archangelum, beatum Joannem Baptistam, sanctos Apostolos Petrum et Paulum, omnes Sanctos, et te, pater, orare pro me ad Dominum Deum nostrum. (at Mass)
    I confess to almighty God, to blessed Mary always virgin, to blessed Michael the Archangel, to blessed John the Baptist, to holy Apostles Peter and Paul, to all saints, and to you, father, that I have sinned excessively in thought, word, and deed, with my fault, my fault, my greatest fault. Therefore I ask blessed Mary always virgin, blessed Michael the Archangel, blessed John the Baptist, holy Apostles Peter and Paul, all saints, and you, father, to pray for me towards the Lord our God.

Chapter Eight

1. Diliges Dominum Deum tuum ex toto corde tuo, et ex tota anima tua, et ex tota fortitudine tua. (Dt.6:5)
   You shall love the Lord your God out of all your heart, and out of all your soul, and out of all your strength.

2. Secundum nomen tuum, Deus, sic et laus tua in fines terrae; justitia plena est dextera tua. (Ps.47:11)
   According to your name, O God, thus also your praise into the ends of the earth; your right hand is full with justice.

3. Domine, inclina caelos tuos, et descende. (Ps.143:5)
   O Lord, incline your heavens and descend.

4. Dominus illuminat caecos… Dominus diligit justos. (Ps.145:8)
   The Lord illuminates the blind, the Lord loves the just.

5. Laudate eum, omnes angeli ejus; laudate eum, omnes virtutes ejus. Laudate eum, sol et luna; laudate eum, omnes stellae et lumen. (Ps.148:2-3)
   Praise him, all his angels; praise him, all his virtues; praise him, sun and moon; praise him, all stars and light!

6. Benedicite, maria et flumina, Domino: laudate et superexaltate eum in saecula. (Dan.3:78)
   Seas and rivers, bless the Lord: praise and highly exalt him into the ages!

7. Qui credit in Filium, habet vitam aeternam; qui autem incredulus est Filio, non videbit vitam, sed ira Dei manet super eum. (Jn.3:36)
   He who believes in the Son has eternal life; however he who is incredulous to the Son will not see life, but the anger of God remains over him.

8. Christus vincit, Christus regnat, Christus imperat. (Christus Rex Antiphon)
   Christ conquers, Christ reigns, Christ reigns as emperor.

9. Obsculta, o fili, praecepta magistri, et inclina aurem cordis tui. (beginning of the *Rule of St. Benedict*)
   Listen carefully, O son, to the commands of the teacher, and incline the ear of your heart.

10. Tua me sapientia dirige. (Clement XI)
    Guide me with your wisdom.

11. Gemma caelestis pretiosa regis. (Peter Damian about St. Benedict)
    A precious gem of the heavenly king.

12. Domine Jesu Christe, Fili Dei vivi, pone Passionem, Crucem, et Mortem tuam inter judicium tuum et animam meam, nunc et in hora mortis meae. (Gregory the Great)
    O Lord Jesus Christ, Son of the living God, put your Passion, Cross, and Death between your judgment and my soul, now and in the hour of my death.

13. Difficile est longum subito deponere amorem. (Catullus)
    It is difficult to suddenly put down a long love.

14. Video sed non credo. (Caspar Hofmann)
    I see but I do not believe.

15. Vincite virtute vera. (Plautus)
    Conquer with true virtue.

16. Vivit et vivet per omnium saeculorum memoriam. (Velleius Paterculus)
    He lives and will live through the memory of all ages.

17. Experto credite. (Virgil)
    Believe the expert.

18. Omnia vincit amor. (Virgil)
    Love conquers all things.

19. Agnus vincet (episcopal motto)
    The Lamb will conquer.

20. Amore omnia vincit (episcopal motto)
    He conquers all things with love.

21. Tua luce dirige (episcopal motto)
    Guide with your light.

22. Vincit omnia veritas (motto of Augusta State University, GA)
    Truth conquers all things.

23. Vincere est vivere (motto of Captain John Smith)
    To conquer is to live.

24. Veritas cum libertate (motto of Winthrop University)
    Truth with liberty

25. Age quod agis. (Latin Proverb)
    Do what you do.

26. Exaltabo te, Deus meus rex, et benedicam nomini tuo in saeculum, et in saeculum saeculi. Per singulos dies benedicam tibi, et laudabo nomen tuum in saeculum, et in saeculum saeculi. Magnus Dominus, et laudabilis nimis, et magnitudinis ejus non est finis. Generatio et generatio laudabit opera tua, et potentiam tuam pronuntiabunt. (Ps.144:1-4)
    I will exalt you, O God my king, and I will bless your name into the age, and into the age of the age. Through single days I will bless you, and I will praise your name into the age, and into the age of the age. Great is the Lord, and excessively laudable, and of his greatness there is not an end. Generation and generation will praise your deeds and will pronounce your power.

27. Benedicite, omnia opera Domini, Domino: laudate et superexaltate eum in saecula. Benedicite, angeli Domini, Domino: laudate et superexaltate eum in saecula. Benedicite, caeli, Domino: laudate et superexaltate eum in saecula. Benedicite, aquae omnes, quae super caelos sunt, Domino: laudate et superexaltate eum in saecula. Benedicite, omnes virtutes Domini, Domino: laudate et superexaltate eum in saecula. Benedicite, sol et luna, Domino: laudate et superexaltate eum in saecula. Benedicite, stellae caeli, Domino: laudate et superexaltate eum in saecula. (Dan.3:57-63)
Bless the Lord, all works of the Lord: praise and highly exalt him into the ages. Bless the Lord, O angels of the Lord: praise and highly exalt him into the ages. Bless the Lord, O heavens: praise and highly exalt him into the ages. Bless the Lord, all waters which are above the heavens: praise and highly exalt him into the ages. Bless the Lord, all virtues of the Lord: praise and highly exalt him into the ages. Bless the Lord, sun and moon: praise and highly exalt him into the ages. Bless the Lord, stars of heaven: praise and highly exalt him into the ages.

28. Benedicite, filii hominum, Domino: laudate et superexaltate eum in saecula... Benedicite, sacerdotes Domini, Domino: laudate et superexaltate eum in saecula. Benedicite, servi Domini, Domino: laudate et superexaltate eum in saecula. Benedicite, spiritus et animae justorum, Domino: laudate et superexaltate eum in saecula. Benedicite, sancti et humiles corde, Domino: laudate et superexaltate eum in saecula. (Dan.3:82, 84-87)
Bless the Lord, O sons of humans: praise and highly exalt him into the ages. Bless the Lord, O priests of the Lord: praise and highly exalt him into the ages. Bless the Lord, O servants of the Lord: praise and highly exalt him into the ages. Bless the Lord, O spirits and souls of the just: praise and highly exalt him into the ages. Bless the Lord, O holy and humble with (regards to the) heart: praise and highly exalt him into the ages.

29. Gloria in excelsis Deo et in terra pax hominibus bonae voluntatis. Laudamus te, benedicimus te, adoramus te, glorificamus te, gratias agimus tibi propter magnam gloriam tuam, Domine Deus, Rex caelestis, Deus Pater omnipotens. Domine Fili unigenite, Jesu Christe, Domine Deus, Agnus Dei, Filius Patris, qui tollis peccata mundi, miserere nobis; qui tollis peccata mundi, suscipe deprecationem nostram. Qui sedes ad dexteram Patris, miserere nobis. Quoniam tu solus Sanctus, tu solus Dominus, tu solus Altissimus, Jesu Christe, cum Sancto Spiritu: in gloria Dei Patris. Amen. (at Mass)
Glory to God in the highests, and on earth peace to humans of good will. We praise you, we bless you, we adore you, we glorify you, we give thanks to you because of your great glory, O Lord God, heavenly king, God almighty Father. O Lord, only-begotten Son, Jesus Christ, Lord God, the Lamb of God, the Son of the Father, you who take away the sins of the world, have mercy on us; you who take away the sins of the world, receive our prayer. You who sit towards the right hand of the Father, have mercy on us. Because you alone are the Holy One, you alone are the Lord, you alone are the Highest One, Jesus Christ, with the Holy Spirit, in the glory of God the Father. Amen.

Chapter Nine

1. Custodi animam meam. (Ps.24:20)
   Guard my soul.

2. Venite, et videte opera Dei. (Ps.65:5)
   Come and see the works of God.

3. Inclina, Domine, aurem tuam et exaudi me. (Ps.85:1)
   Incline your ear, O Lord, and listen to me.

4. Consilium custodiet te, et prudentia servabit te. (Prv.2:11)
   Counsel will guard you, and prudence will preserve you.

5. Beatus homo qui invenit sapientiam. (Prv.3:13)
   Blessed is the human who finds wisdom.

6. Audiet me Deus meus (Mic.7:7)
   My God will hear me.

7. Qui autem facit voluntatem Dei manet in aeternum. (1Jn.2:17)
   However, he who does the will of God remains into eternity.

8. Benedictus qui venit in nomine Domini. Hosanna in excelsis. (at Mass)
   Blessed is he who comes in the name of the Lord. Hosanna in the highests.

9. Domine labia mea aperies; et os meum annunciabit laudem tuam. (at the Divine Office)
   O Lord, you will open my lips, and my mouth will announce your praise.

10. Boni angeli semper nos custodiunt. (Aquinas)
    Good angels always guard us.

11. Ex nihilo nihil fit. (Aquinas)
    Nothing becomes out of nothing.

12. Gratia non tollit naturam sed perficit. (Aquinas)
    Grace does not take away nature but perfects [it].

13. Quocumque fugies, Deus te videbit. (Augustine)
    Wheresoever you will flee, God will see you.

14. Ecce, vox sanguinis fratris nostri Jesu clamat ad te de cruce: exaudi, Domine! (Cajetan)
    Behold, the voice of the blood of our brother Jesus calls towards you down from the Cross: hear clearly, O Lord!

15. Veni et suscipe me. (a Kempis)
    Come and support me.

16. Arma virumque cano. (beginning of Virgil's *Aeneid*)
    I sing about weapons and a man.

17. Aut viam inveniam aut faciam. (Hannibal)
    Either I will find a way or I will make [one].

18. Orbis non sufficit. (Juvenal)
    The world does not suffice.

19. Necessitas etiam timidos fortes facit. (Sallust)
    Necessity makes timid men also strong.

20. Sed fugit interea, fugit irreparabile tempus. (Virgil)
    But meanwhile irrecoverable time flees, flees!

21. Aperiet coelum (episcopal motto)
    Heaven will open.

22. Aperite portas Christo (episcopal motto)
    Open the gates to Christ!

23. Aperite portas Redemptori (episcopal motto)
    Open the gates to the Redeemer!

24. Fac et vives (episcopal motto)
    Do [it] and you will live.

25. Faciam vos fieri piscatores hominum (episcopal motto)
    I will make y'all to become fishers of humans.

26. Sufficit gratia tua (episcopal motto)
    Your grace suffices.

27. Ave maris stella, Dei mater alma, atque semper virgo, felix caeli porta. (*Ave Maris Stella*)
    Hail, Star of the Sea, kind Mother of God, and always virgin, happy gate of heaven.

28. Dormi, Jesu! Mater ridet quae tam dulcem somnum videt. (*Dormi Jesu*)
    Sleep, Jesus! Mother smiles who sees so sweet a sleep.

29. Sancti Angeli, custodes nostri, defendite nos in proelio. (*Little Office of the Guardian Angel*)
    Holy Angels, our guards, defend us in battle.

30. Gaudet chorus caelestium et Angeli canunt Deum, palamque fit pastoribus Pastor, Creator omnium. (Sedulius, *A Solis Ortus*)
    A chorus of heavenly things rejoices, and angels sing about God; it happens openly to shepherds: the Shepherd, Creator of all things.

31. Ave Regina Caelorum. Ave Domina Angelorum. Salve radix, salve porta, ex qua mundo lux est orta. Gaude Virgo gloriosa, super omnes speciosa. Vale, o valde decora, et pro nobis Christum exora. (*Lent Antiphon*)
    Hail Queen of the heavens. Hail Lady of the angels. Hello root, hello gate, out of whom a light is arisen to the world. Rejoice, glorious virgin, lovely above all persons. Goodbye, O very honored one, and pray fervently to Christ for us.

Chapter Ten

1. Veni in terram quam monstrabo tibi. Faciamque te in gentem magnam, et benedicam tibi, et magnificabo nomen tuum, erisque benedictus. (Gen.12:1-2)
   Come into the land which I will show to you. And I will make you into a great nation, and I will bless you, and I will make your name great, and you will be blessed.

2. Tolle filium tuum unigenitum, quem diligis, Isaac, et vade in terram visionis. (Gen.22:2)
   Take up your son, the only-begotten one, whom you love, Isaac, and go into the land of vision (i.e. that I will show you).

3. Dirige me in veritate tua, et doce me. (Ps.24:5)
   Guide me in your truth and teach me.

4. Beatus es, et bene tibi erit. (Ps.127:2)
   You are blessed, and it will be well to you.

5. Pulchra es, amica mea; suavis, et decora sicut Jerusalem. (SS.6:3)
   You are beautiful, my girlfriend; pleasant, and adorned like Jerusalem.

6. In principio erat Verbum, et Verbum erat apud Deum, et Deus erat Verbum. (Jn.1:1)
   In the beginning was the Word, and the Word was at God, and God was the Word.

7. Lux sum mundi. (Jn.9:5)
   I am the light of the world.

8. Domine, non sum dignus. (at Mass)
   O Lord, I am not worthy.

9. Date ergo pauperibus. (Augustine)
   Therefore, give to the poor.

10. Etsi homines falles Deum tamen non fallere poteris. (Augustine)
    Even if you will deceive humans, nevertheless you will not be able to deceive God.

11. Nova sunt quae dicitis, mira sunt quae dicitis, falsa sunt quae dicitis. (Augustine)
    New things are that which you say, marvelous things are that which you say, false things are that which you say.

12. Spiritus sapientiae… dicit: Ecce, adsum. (Bernard)
    The spirit of wisdom says: behold, I am present.

13. Videre poteris Deum per te tanquam per imaginem. (Bonaventure)
    You will be able to see God through yourself just as through an image.

14. Habere non potest Deum patrem qui Ecclesiam non habet matrem. (Cyprian)
    He is not able to have God as father who does not have the Church as mother.

15. Cogito ergo sum. (Descartes)
    I think therefore I am.

16. Vivere est cogitare. (Cicero)
    To live is to think.

17. Non sum qualis eram. (Horace)
    I am not as I was.

18. Pulvis et umbra sumus. (Horace)
    We are dust and a shadow.

19. Mens sana in corpore sano. (Juvenal)
    A healthy mind in a healthy body.

20. Homines dum docent discunt. (Seneca)
    Humans learn while they teach.

21. Mens regnum bona possidet. (Seneca)
    A good mind possesses a kingdom.

22. Qualis dominus, talis et servus. (Petronius)
    As the lord, so also the servant.

23. Amicitia semper prodest. (Seneca)
    Friendship is always beneficial.

24. Non omnia possumus omnes. (Virgil)
    We are not all able [to be] all things.

25. Adesse festinant tempora (episcopal motto)
    The times hurry to be present.

26. Domini sumus (episcopal motto)
    We are of the Lord.

27. Deus adest et vocat te. (said to John Paul the Great when he was elected Pope but had yet to accept.)
    God is present and calls you.

28. Vade in pace! (Roman farewell)
    Go in peace.

29. Benedictus es, Domine Deus patrum nostrorum: et laudabilis, et gloriosus, et superexaltatus in saecula. Et benedictum nomen gloriae tuae sanctum: et laudabile, et superexaltatum in omnibus saeculis. Benedictus es in templo sancto gloriae tuae: et superlaudabilis, et supergloriosus in saecula. Benedictus es in throno regni tui: et superlaudabilis, et superexaltatus in saecula. Benedictus es qui intueris abyssos et sedes super cherubim: et laudabilis, et superexaltatus in saecula. Benedictus es in firmamento caeli: et laudabilis et gloriosus in saecula. (Dan.3:52-56)
    Blessed are you, O Lord God of our fathers: also laudable, and glorious, and highly exalted into the ages. And blessed is the holy name of your glory: also laudable, and highly exalted in all the ages. Blessed are you in the holy temple of your glory: and highly laudable and highly glorious into the ages. Blessed are you on the throne of your kingdom: and highly laudable and highly exalted into the ages. Blessed are you who look upon the abysses and who sit over the cherubim: also laudable and highly exalted into the ages. Blessed are you in the firmament of heaven: also laudable and glorious into the ages.

Chapter Eleven

1. Apud te est fons vitae, et in lumine tuo videbimus lumen. (Ps.35:10)
   At you is the fountain of life, and in your light we will see light.

2. In memoria aeterna erit justus… paratum cor ejus sperare in Domino. (Ps.111:7)
   The just will be in eternal memory: his heart having been prepared to hope in the Lord.

3. Sanctus, Sanctus, Sanctus Dominus Deus omnipotens, qui erat, et qui est, et qui venturus est. (Rev.4:8)
   Holy, holy, holy Lord God almighty, who was, and who is, and who is about to come.

4. Veni, Sanctificator omnipotens aeterne Deus, et benedic hoc sacrificium tuo sancto nomini praeparatum. (at Mass)
   Come, Sanctifier almighty eternal God, and bless this sacrifice having been prepared to your holy name.

5. Deus, in adjutorium meum intende. (at the Divine Office)
   God, focus into my help.

6. Da mihi, Deus meus, cor meum ad te dirigere. (Aquinas)
   Give to me, my God, that my heart be guided towards you.

7. In medio stat virtus. (Aquinas)
   Virtue stands in the middle.

8. Intelligo me intelligere. (Augustine)
   I understand myself to understand.

9. Mors est poena peccati. (Augustine)
   Death is the punishment of sin.

10. Quantum in te crescit amor, tantum crescit pulchritudo; quia ipsa caritas est animae pulchritudo. (Augustine)
    How great love grows in you, so great grows beauty; because the love itself is the beauty of a soul.

11. Dulce bellum inexpertis. (Erasmus)
    War is sweet to inexperienced people.

12. O Jerusalem aurea civitas, ornata Regis purpura! (Hildegard)
    O Jerusalem, golden city, adorned with the purple of the King!

13. Dictum factumque facit frux. (Ennius)
    The result makes (determines) the thing having been said and done.

14. Nemo liber est qui corpori servit. (Seneca)
    No one is free who serves the body.

15. Discite justitiam moniti. (Virgil)
    Learn justice, O you having been warned!

16. Nec mora, nec requies. (Virgil)
    Neither delay, nor rest.

17. Semper apertus (motto of the University of Heidelberg)
    Always having been opened

18. Factum fieri infectum non potest. (Latin Proverb)
    The thing having been done is not able to become undone.

19. Monstra te esse matrem. (*Ave Maris Stella*)
    Show yourself to be a mother.

20. Virgo singularis, inter omnes mitis, nos culpis solutos, mites fac et castos. (*Ave Maris Stella*)
    Singular virgin, among all meek, make us, freed with (from) faults, meek and chaste.

21. Sancte… venture Judex saeculi! (*Conditor Alme Siderum*)
    O holy Judge of the age, about to come!

22. Quantus tremor est futurus, quando Judex est venturus, cuncta stricte discussurus! (*Dies Irae*)
    How great a tremor is about to be, when the Judge is about to come, about to shatter all things strictly!

23. Mater amata… ora, ora pro nobis. (*O Sanctissima*)
    Loved mother, pray, pray for us.

24. Arbor decora et fulgida, ornata Regis purpura, electa digno stipite, tam sancta membra tangere. (Venantius Fortunatus, *Vexilla Regis*)
    Honored and shining tree, adorned with the purple of the King, chosen with (from) a worthy tree trunk to touch so holy limbs.

25. Veni veni Emmanuel, captivum solve Israel, qui gemit in exilio, privatus Dei Filio. (*Veni Veni Emmanuel*)
    Come, come, O Emmanuel, release captive Israel who groans in exile, deprived of the Son of God.

26. Mors et vita duello… dux vitae mortuus, regnat vivus. (Wipo of Burgundy, *Victimae Paschali*)
    Death and life are with (at) war: the leader of life is dead--he reigns alive!

Chapter Twelve

1. Dominus Deus tuus ignis consumens est. (Dt.4:24)
   The Lord your God is a consuming fire.

2. Firmamentum est Dominus timentibus eum. (Ps.24:14)
   The Lord is a support to those fearing him.

3. Credo videre bona Domini in terra viventium. (Ps.26:13)
   I believe [myself] to see the good things of the Lord in the land of the living.

4. Parabolae Salomonis, filii David, regis Israel, ad sciendam sapientiam et disciplinam: Timor Domini principium sapientiae. (Prv.1:1-2, 7)
   Parables of Solomon, son of David, king of Israel, in order to know wisdom and discipline: fear of the Lord is the beginning of wisdom.

5. Inclina cor tuum ad cognoscendam prudentiam. (Prv.2:2)
   Incline your heart in order to recognize prudence.

6. Gloriam sapientes possidebunt. (Prv.3:35)
   Wise people will possess glory.

7. Benedicite, lux et tenebrae, Domino: laudate et superexaltate eum in saecula. (Dan.3:72)
   Bless the Lord, O light and shadows: praise and highly exalt him into the ages.

8. Non est Deus mortuorum, sed viventium. (Mt.22:32)
   God is not of the dead, but of the living.

9. Domine, ad adjuvandum me, festina. (at the Divine Office)
   O Lord, hurry in order to help me!

10. O Oriens, splendor lucis aeternae, et sol justitiae: veni, et illumina sedentes in tenebris, et umbra mortis. (Advent Antiphon)
    O rising sun, splendor of eternal light and sun of justice: come and illuminate those sitting in the shadows and the shadow of death.

11. O Emmanuel, rex et legifer noster, exspectatio gentium, et salvator earum: veni ad salvandum nos, Domine, Deus noster. (Advent Antiphon)
    O Emmanuel, our king and law-giver, expectation of the nations and savior of them: come in order to save us, O Lord our God.

12. Nec audiendi qui solent dicere, "vox populi vox Dei." (Alcuin)
    Neither are they to be listened to who are used to say, "the voice of the people is the voice of God."

13. Amo te, Redemptor meus, amo te, Deus meus, ad nihil aspiro nisi ad amandum te ex toto corde meo. (Alphonsus Liguori)
    I love you, my Redeemer, I love you, my God, I aspire towards nothing except in order to love you out of all my heart.

14. Cantare amantis est. (Augustine)
    To sing is of a lover.

15. Ecclesia semper reformanda est. (Augustine)
    The Church must always be reformed.

16. Tolle, lege. (said by the Holy Spirit to Augustine at his conversion)
    Take up, read.

17. Angeli Deo ministrantes Deum in humanitate vident. (Hildegard)
    The angels ministering to God see God in humanity.

18. Spiritus Sanctus vivificans vita, movens omnia, et radix es in omni creatura; et sic es fulgens ac laudabilis vita, suscitans et resuscitans omnia. (Hildegard)
    You are the Holy Spirit, making life alive, moving all things, and the root in every creature. And thus you are glistening and laudable life, awakening and reawakening all things.

19. Quanta nunc mihi et omni populo Christiano habenda est devotio et reverentia in praesentia Sacramenti! (a Kempis)
    How great devotion and reverence must now be had by me and every Christian people in the presence of the Sacrament!

20. Omnia autem quae secundum naturam fiunt sunt habenda in bonis. (Cicero)
    However all things which happen according to nature must be had in the good things.

21. Nil desperandum. (Horace)
    Nothing must be despaired of.

22. Ajunt enim multum legendum esse, non multa. (Pliny)
    For they say much must be read, not many.

23. Sapiens vivit quantum debet, non quantum potest. (Seneca)
    The wise man lives how much he ought, not how much he can.

24. Audentes fortuna juvat. (Virgil)
    Fortune helps the daring.

25. Ad docendum Christi mysteria (episcopal motto)
    In order to teach the mysteries of Christ

26. Ad serviendum (episcopal motto)
    In order to serve

27. Audiens et proclamans (episcopal motto)
    Hearing and proclaiming

28. Aurora consurgens (episcopal motto)
    Dawn is rising.

29. Auxiliante Deo (episcopal motto)
    With God helping

30. Gloria Dei homo vivens (episcopal motto)
    The glory of God is a human living.

31. Semper ardens (motto of Carl Jacobsen)
    Always burning

32. Deo juvante (motto of Monaco)
    With God helping

33. Semper ascendens (motto of Nuevo Leon)
    Always ascending

34. Ignis ardens (Pius X according to St. Malachy)
    A burning fire

35. Super omnes angelos pura, immaculata, atque ad regis dexteram stans! (*Little Office of the Immaculate Conception*)
    Above all the angels, pure, immaculate, and standing towards the right hand of the king.

36. Mater gratiae, dulcis spes reorum, fulgens stella maris! (*Little Office of the Immaculate Conception*)
    Mother of grace, sweet hope of the guilty, glistening star of the sea!

37. Jesu dulcis memoria, dans vera cordis gaudia: sed super mel et omnia ejus dulcis praesentia. (Bernard, *Jesu Dulcis Memoria*)
    O Jesus, sweet memory, giving true joys of heart: but his presence is sweet above honey and all things.

38. Jesu, dulcedo cordium, fons vivus, lumen mentium, excedens omne gaudium et omne desiderium. (Bernard, *Jesu Dulcis Memoria*)
    Jesus, sweetness of hearts, living fountain, light of minds, exceeding every joy and every desire.

39. Rex tremendae majestatis, qui salvandos salvas gratis, salva me, fons pietatis. (*Dies Irae*)
    King of tremendous majesty, you who save freely those about to be saved, save me, fountain of piety.

40. Ave, in triumphis Filii, in ignibus Paracliti, in regni honore et lumine, Regina fulgens gloria. (Augustine Thomas Ricchini, *Te Gestientem Gaudiis*)
    Hail, in the triumphs of the Son, in the fires of the Paraclete, in the honor and light of the kingdom, O Queen glistening with glory!

Chapter Thirteen

1. Num custos fratris mei sum ego? (Gen.4:9)
   Surely I am not the guard of my brother?

2. Sancti eritis, quia ego sanctus sum. (Lev.11:45)
   You shall be holy, because I am holy.

3. Custodite mandata mea, et facite ea. Ego Dominus. (Lev.22:31)
   Guard my commands and do them. I am the Lord.

4. Invocabuntque nomen meum super filios Israel, et ego benedicam eis. (Num.6:27)
   And they will invoke my name over the sons of Israel, and I will bless them.

5. Dominus virtutum nobiscum; susceptor noster Deus Jacob. (Ps.45:12)
   The Lord of virtues is with us; our supporter is the God of Jacob.

6. Regnabit Deus super gentes; Deus sedet super sedem sanctam suam. (Ps.46:9)
   God will reign over the nations; God sits on his own holy seat.

7. Tu es sacerdos in aeternum secundum ordinem Melchisedech. (Ps.109:4)
   You are a priest into eternity according to the order of Melchizedek.

8. Gloria filiorum patres eorum. (Prv.17:6)
   The glory of sons is their fathers.

9. Tu vero Deum time. (Ecc.5:6)
   You, truly: fear God!

10. Nescit homo finem suum. (Ecc.9:12)
    A human does not know his own end.

11. Ego dilecto meo, et dilectus meus mihi. (SS.6:2)
    I am to my loved one, and my loved one is to me.

12. Rex Israel Dominus in medio tui. (Zeph.3:15)
    The King of Israel, the Lord, is in the midst of you.

13. Vos estis lux mundi. (Mt.5:14)
    Y'all are the light of the world.

14. Non est discipulus super magistrum, nec servus super dominum suum. (Mt.10:24)
    A student is not above the teacher, nor is a servant above his own lord.

15. Quia non est propheta sine honore nisi in patria sua. (Mk.6:4)
    Because a prophet is not without honor except in his own homeland.

16. Vos vero quem me esse dicitis? Respondens Petrus, ait ei: Tu es Christus. (Mk.8:29)
    Truly, whom do y'all say me to be? Peter, responding, says to him: You are the Christ.

17. Ecce enim regnum Dei intra vos est. (Lk.17:21)
    For behold, the kingdom of God is within y'all.

18. Amen, amen dico vobis: qui credit in me, habet vitam aeternam. Ego sum panis vitae. (Jn.6:47-48)
    Amen, amen I say to y'all, he who believes in me has eternal life. I am the bread of life.

19. Ego sum lux mundi. (Jn.8:12)
    I am the light of the world.

20. Veritas liberabit vos. (Jn.8:32)
    The truth will liberate y'all.

21. Ego sum pastor bonus. (Jn.10:14)
    I am the good shepherd.

22. Ego sum via, et veritas, et vita. Nemo venit ad Patrem, nisi per me. (Jn.14:6)
    I am the way, and the truth, and the life. No one comes towards the Father except through me.

23. Qui diligit fratrem suum, in lumine manet. (1Jn.2:10)
    He who loves his own brother remains in the light.

24. Ego sum alpha et omega, principium et finis, dicit Dominus Deus: qui est, et qui erat, et qui venturus est, omnipotens. (Rev.1:8)
    I am the alpha and the omega, the beginning and the end, says the Lord God: who is, and who was, and who is about to come, the almighty.

25. Gratia Domini nostri Jesu Christi cum omnibus vobis. Amen. (Rev.22:21)
    The grace of our Lord Jesus Christ be with you all. Amen.

26. Dominus tecum. (at Mass)
    The Lord be with you.

27. Dominus vobiscum. (at Mass)
    The Lord be with y'all.

28. Per Dominum nostrum Jesum Christum, filium tuum, qui tecum vivit et regnat in unitate Spiritus Sancti Deus, per omnia saecula saeculorum. (at Mass)
    Through our Lord Jesus Christ, your Son, who with you lives and reigns in the unity of the Holy Spirit: God through all the ages of ages.

29. Ego te absolvo. (in Confession)
    I absolve you.

30. Ecce Dominus veniet, et omnes Sancti ejus cum eo: et erit in die illa lux magna. (Advent Antiphon)
    Behold, the Lord will come, and all his holy ones with him: and there will be on that day a great light.

31. Deus meus, tu omnipotens es, effice me sanctum. (Alphonsus Liguori)
    My God, you are almighty: make me holy.

32. O Deus ego amo te! (Francis Xavier)
    O God, I love you!

33. O tu illustrata de Divina claritate, clara Virgo Maria, Verbo Dei infusa! (Hildegard)
    O you having been illustrated down from Divine clarity, O renowned Virgin Mary, having been infused with the Word of God!

34. Pasce me, Domine, et pasce mecum. (John Damascene)
    Shepherd me, Lord, and shepherd with me.

35. Ecce ego venio ad te, Domine. (a Kempis)
    Behold, I come towards you, Lord.

36. Et ecce tu praesens es hic apud me in altari, Deus meus, Sanctus Sanctorum, hominum Creator et Dominus Angelorum. (a Kempis)
    And behold, you are present here at me on the altar, my God, Holy of Holies, Creator of humans and Lord of angels.

37. Non tu pervenis ad Christum, sed Christus pervenit ad te. (Sedulius)
    You do not come through towards Christ, but Christ comes through towards you.

38. Nil igitur mors est ad nos. (Lucretius)
    Therefore, death is nothing towards us.

39. Sic ego nec sine te nec tecum vivere possum. (Ovid)
    Thus I am able to live neither without you nor with you.

40. Sacer intra nos spiritus sedet, malorum bonorumque nostrorum observator et custos. (Seneca)
    A holy spirit sits within us, the guard and observer of our bad and good [deeds].

41. Non mihi Domine (episcopal motto)
    Not to me, O Lord

42. Sufficit tibi gratia mea (episcopal motto)
    My grace suffices to you.

43. Tecum et tibi Jesu (episcopal motto)
    With you and to you, O Jesus

44. Semper eadem (motto of Elizabeth I of England)
    Always the same

45. Semper idem (motto of the Underberg company)
    Always the same

46. Tu autem Domine miserere nobis. (after readings in Catholic liturgies)
    You, however, O Lord: have mercy on us.

47. Id est (commonly abbreviated as *i.e.*)
    It is.

48. Angele Dei, qui custos es mei, me tibi commissum pietate superna, illumina, custodi, rege, et guberna. (*Angele Dei*)
Angel of God, you who are a guard of me, illumine, guard, rule, and govern me having been committed to you with heavenly piety.

49. Jesu Christe crucifixe, miserere mei! (Franciscan Way of the Cross)
O Jesus Christ having been crucified, have mercy on me!

50. Tu Trinitatis gloria, in te Patris sunt gaudia, jungit tibi se Filius, in te quiescit Spiritus. (*Little Office of the Sacred Heart of Jesus*)
You are the glory of the Trinity, in you are the joys of the Father, the Son joins himself to you, in you the Spirit rests.

51. Bone pastor, panis vere, Jesu, nostri miserere. (Aquinas, *Ecce Panis Angelorum*)
Good shepherd, true bread, Jesus, having mercy on us.

52. Tu nos bona fac videre, in terra viventium. (Aquinas, *Ecce Panis Angelorum*)
You: make us to see good things in the land of the living.

53. Mane nobiscum, Domine, et nos illustra lumine. (Bernard, *Jesu Dulcis Memoria*)
Remain with us, Lord, and illustrate us with light.

54. Praesta Pater omnipotens, per Jesum Christum Dominum, qui tecum in perpetuum, regnat cum Sancto Spiritu. (*Te Lucis ante Terminum*)
Stand in front, O Father almighty, through Jesus Christ the Lord, who with you in perpetuity reigns with the Holy Spirit.

55. Libera nos, salva nos, vivifica nos, O Beata Trinitas! (*Trisagium Angelicum*)
Free us, save us, make us alive, O blessed Trinity!

Chapter Fourteen

1. Ecce sic benedicetur homo qui timet Dominum. (Ps.127:4)
Behold, thus will be blessed the human who fears the Lord.

2. Ecce virgo concipiet et pariet filium, et vocabitur nomen ejus Emmanuel. (Isa.7:14)
Behold, the virgin will conceive and give birth to a son, and his name will be called Emmanuel.

3. Beati pacifici: quoniam filii Dei vocabuntur. (Mt.5:9)
Blessed are the peacemakers: because they will be called sons of God.

4. Petite, et dabitur vobis: quaerite, et invenietis: pulsate, et aperietur vobis. Omnis enim qui petit, accipit: et qui quaerit, invenit: et pulsanti aperietur. (Mt.7:7-8)
   Ask, and it will be given to y'all; seek, and y'all will find; knock, and it will be opened to y'all. For everyone who asks, receives, and he who seeks, finds, and it will be opened to the one knocking.

5. Cupio dissolvi et vivere cum Christo. (Phil.1:23)
   I desire to be dissolved and to live with Christ.

6. O sacrum convivium, in quo Christus sumitur: recolitur memoria Passionis ejus: mens impletur gratia: et futurae gloriae nobis pignus datur. (Aquinas, *Corpus Christi Antiphon*)
   O sacred banquet, in which Christ is received; the memory of his Passion is recalled, the mind is filled with grace, and a pledge of future glory is given to us.

7. Bene curris, sed extra viam. (Augustine)
   You run well, but outside the way.

8. Ecce intus eras et ego foris, et ibi te quaerebam. (Augustine)
   Behold, you were within and I outside, and there I was seeking you.

9. Non intratur in veritatem nisi in caritatem. (Augustine)
   One does not enter into truth except into charity.

10. Salus extra Ecclesiam non est. (Augustine)
    There is not salvation outside the Church.

11. Ora pro nobis ad tuum Natum, stella maris, Maria. (Hildegard)
    Pray for us towards your one-having-been-born, O star of the sea, Mary.

12. Quomodo potest demonstrari, quod videri non potest? (Hugo of St. Victor)
    How it is able to be demonstrated, which is not able to be seen?

13. Nos numerus sumus et fruges consumere nati. (Horace)
    We are a number and born to consume produce.

14. Fas est et ab hoste doceri. (Ovid)
    It is okay to be taught also by an enemy.

15. Certa amittimus dum incerta petimus. (Plautus)
    We send away the certain while we seek the uncertain.

16. Nemo autem regere potest nisi qui et regi. (Seneca)
    However no one is able to rule except he who also [is able] to be ruled.

17. Possunt quia posse videntur. (Virgil)
    They are able because they are seen to be able.

18. Stat crux dum volvitur orbis. (Carthusian motto)
    The Cross stands while the world is turned around.

19. Alma Matre ducor (episcopal motto)
    I am led by a kind Mother.

20. Amor non amatur (episcopal motto)
    Love is not loved.

21. In Jerusalem consolabimini (episcopal motto)
    In Jerusalem y'all will be consoled.

22. Turris fortis mihi Deus. (motto of the Irish Kelly Clan)
    God is a strong tower to me.

23. Non ducor, duco (motto of Sao Paulo)
    I am not led, I lead.

24. Ex peccato peccatum nascitur. (Latin Proverb)
    Out of sin, sin is born.

25. Tempora mutantur, et nos mutamur in illis. (Latin Proverb)
    The times are changed, and we are changed in them.

26. Veritas laborare potest, vinci non potest. (Latin Proverb)
    Truth is able to labor, it is not able to be conquered.

27. Emitte Spiritum tuum et creabuntur, et renovabis faciem terrae. (Catholic Prayer)
    Send out your Spirit and they will be created, and you will renew the face of the earth.

28. Per signum Crucis de inimicis nostris libera nos, Deus noster. (Catholic Prayer)
    Through the sign of the Cross, down from our enemies free us, O our God!

29. Orbi salus tu perdito. (*Little Office of the Sacred Heart of Jesus*)
    You are salvation to a ruined world.

30. Angelum nobis medicum salutis mitte de caelis Raphael. (*Christe Sanctorum*)
    Send to us the medical angel of salvation down from the heavens: Raphael.

31. Ad astra Virgo tollitur. (*Jam Morte Victor Obruta*)
    Towards the stars the Virgin is taken up.

32. Gaude, gaude, Emmanuel nascetur pro te Israel. (*Veni Veni Emmanuel*)
    Rejoice, rejoice, Emmanuel will be born for you, O Israel.

Chapter Fifteen

1. Quid est homo, quia magnificas eum? (Job.7:17)
   What is a human, that you magnify him?

2. Quis est homo qui timet Dominum? (Ps.24:12)
   Who is the human who fears the Lord?

3. Quis est homo qui vivet et non videbit mortem? (Ps.88:49)
   Who is the human who will live and will not see death?

4. Rogate quae ad pacem sunt Jerusalem: et abundantia diligentibus te. (Ps.121:6)
   Ask for those things which are towards the peace of Jerusalem: also abundance to those loving you.

5. Quem enim diligit Dominus, corripit. (Prv.3:12)
   For him whom the Lord loves, he disciplines.

6. Quis non timebit te, O Rex gentium? (Jer.10:7)
   Who will not fear you, O King of the nations?

7. Non omnis qui dicit mihi, Domine, Domine, intrabit in regnum caelorum: sed qui facit voluntatem Patris mei, qui in caelis est. (Mt.7:21)
   Not everyone who says to me, Lord, Lord, will enter into the kingdom of the heavens, but he who does the will of my Father who is in the heavens.

8. Quid autem vocatis me Domine Domine et non facitis quae dico? (Lk.6:46)
   However, what--y'all call me Lord, Lord, and do not do those things which I say?

9. Pater dimitte illis non enim sciunt quid faciunt. (Lk.23:24)
   Father, forgive them for they do not know what they are doing.

10. Deus caritas est: et qui manet in caritate, in Deo manet, et Deus in eo. (1Jn.4:16)
    God is love, and he who remains in love, remains in God, and God in him.

11. Quis est, qui vincit mundum, nisi qui credit quoniam Jesus est Filius Dei? (1Jn.5:5)
    Who is it who conquers the world except he who believes that Jesus is the Son of God?

12. …qui vivis et regnas per omnia saecula saeculorum. (Christian Doxology)
    … you who live and reign through all the ages of ages.

13. Israel es tu Rex, Davidis et inclyta proles: nomine qui in Domini, Rex benedicte, venis. (Palm Sunday Antiphon)
    You are the King of Israel and the glorious offspring of David who come in the name of the Lord, O blessed King!

14. O vere beata nox in qua terrenis caelestia, humanis divina junguntur! (Exsultet)
    O truly blessed night in which heavenly things are joined to earthly things, divine things to human things.

15. Homo ordinatur ad Deum sicut ad quendam finem qui comprehensionem rationis excedit. (Aquinas)
    A human is ordered towards God as towards a certain end which exceeds the comprehension of reason.

16. Quidquid fit, causam habet. (Aquinas)
    Whatever happens has a cause.

17. Deus est qui omnem mundum regit. (Augustine)
    God is he who rules all the world.

18. Nescio quod nescio. (Augustine)
    I do not know that which I do not know.

19. Qui bene cantat bis orat. (Augustine)
    He who sings well prays twice.

20. Sum quod sum. (Augustine)
    I am that which I am.

21. Qui me amat, amat et canem meam. (Bernard)
    He who loves me, loves also my dog.

22. Non est solitarius, cum quo est Deus. (Hugo of St. Victor)
    He is not solitary with whom God is.

23. Deus aeterne, cujus natura bonitas et opus misericordia est! (Innocent III)
    O Eternal God, whose nature is goodness and work is mercy!

24. Sed quis ego sum, Domine? (a Kempis)
    But who am I, O Lord?

25. Qui legis, intellige in Domino semper. (Macarius of Alexandria)
    You who read, always understand [it] in the Lord.

26. Dicite gentibus… quod Deus a cruce regnat. (Odo of Cluny)
    Say to the nations that God reigns from the Cross.

27. Faber est suae quisque fortunae. (Appius Claudius Caecus)
    Each is the artisan of his own fortune.

28. Caelum, non animum, mutant qui trans mare currunt. (Horace)
    They change the sky, not the soul, who run across the sea.

29. Cui malus est nemo, quis bonus esse potest? (Martial)
    To whom no one is bad, who is able to be good?

30. Malum est consilium quod mutari non potest. (Publilius Syrus)
    Bad is the counsel which is not able to be changed.

31. Gratia autem Dei sum id quod sum (episcopal motto)
    However with the grace of God I am the thing which I am.

32. Quaecumque sunt vera - motto of Northwestern University
    Whatsoever things are true.

33. Suum cuique (motto of the Order of the Black Eagle)
    To each his own.

34. Quod oculus non videt, cor non desiderat. (Latin Proverb)
    That which the eye does not see, the heart does not desire.

35. Benedic, Domine, nos et haec tua dona quae de tua largitate sumus sumpturi, per Christum Dominum nostrum. Amen. (Catholic Prayer before meals)
    Bless us, O Lord, and these your gifts which we are about to receive down from your abundance through Jesus Christ our Lord. Amen.

36. Agimus tibi gratias, omnipotens Deus, pro universis beneficiis tuis, qui vivis et regnas in saecula saeculorum. Amen. (Catholic Prayer after meals)
    We give to you thanks, almighty God, for your universal good deeds, you who live and reign into the ages of ages. Amen.

37. Ecce Panis angelorum, factus cibus viatorum, vere panis filiorum, non mittendus canibus. (Aquinas, *Ecce Panis Angelorum*)
    Behold the bread of angels, having been made the food of the journeyers, truly the bread of sons, not to be sent to dogs.

38. Sumens illud Ave, Gabrielis ore, funda nos in pace, mutans Evae nomen. (*Ave Maris Stella*)
    Receiving that "Hail" with (from) the mouth of Gabriel, establish us in peace, changing the name of Eve.

39. Qui diceris Paraclitus, donum Dei altissimi, fons vivus, ignis, caritas, et spiritalis unctio. (Rabanus Maurus, *Veni Creator Spiritus*)
    You who are said to be Paraclete, gift of God the highest, living fountain, fire, charity, and spiritual anointing.

Chapter Sixteen

1. In principio creavit Deus caelum et terram. Terra autem erat inanis et vacua, et tenebrae erant super faciem abyssi: et spiritus Dei ferebatur super aquas. (Gen.1:1-2)
   In the beginning God created heaven and earth. However the earth was empty and void, and shadows were over the face of the abyss, and the spirit of God was hovering over the waters.

2. Vocavitque Deus firmamentum Caelum. (Gen.1:8)
   And God called the firmament 'Heaven.'

3. Et creavit Deus hominem ad imaginem suam: ad imaginem Dei creavit illum, masculum et feminam creavit eos. (Gen.1:27)
   And God created the human towards his own image; towards the image of God he created him, male and female he created them.

4. Dixit quoque Dominus Deus: Non est bonum esse hominem solum. (Gen.2:18)
   The Lord God also said, 'It is not good, the human to be alone.'

5. Dixit Deus ad Moysen: Ego sum qui sum. Ait: Sic dices filiis Israel: Qui est, misit me ad vos. (Ex.3:14)
   God said towards Moses: I am who I am. He says, 'Thus you shall say to the sons of Israel: He who is has sent me towards y'all.

6. Ecce ostendit nobis Dominus Deus noster majestatem et magnitudinem suam. (Dt.5:24)
   Behold, the Lord our God has shown to us his own majesty and greatness.

7. Exaudi, Domine, vocem meam, qua clamavi ad te; miserere mei, et exaudi me. (Ps.26:7)
   Hear, O Lord, my voice, with which I have called towards you; have mercy on me and hear me.

8. Benedictus Dominus, quoniam exaudivit vocem deprecationis meae. (Ps.27:6)
   Blessed is the Lord, because he has heard the voice of my prayer.

9. Sicut audivimus, sic vidimus, in civitate Domini virtutum, in civitate Dei nostri. (Ps.47:9)
   As we have heard, thus we have seen, in the city of the Lord of virtues, in the city of our God.

10. Venite, audite, et narrabo, omnes qui timetis Deum, quanta fecit animae meae. (Ps.65:16)
    All y'all who fear God: come, hear, and I will narrate how great things he has done to my soul.

11. Dominus sapientia fundavit terram. (Prv.3:19)
    The Lord has established the earth with wisdom.

12. Verba Ecclesiastae, filii David, regis Jerusalem: Vanitas vanitatum, dixit Ecclesiastes, vanitas vanitatum, et omnia vanitas. (Ecc.1:1-2)
    The words of Ecclesiastes, the son of David, king of Jerusalem: vanity of vanities, said Ecclesiastes, vanity of vanities, and all things are vanity.

13. Dedi cor meum in cunctis operibus quae fiunt sub sole. (Ecc.8:9)
    I have given my heart in all deeds which happen under the sun.

14. Per noctes quaesivi quem diligit anima mea: quaesivi illum, et non inveni. (SS.3:1)
    Through the nights I sought him whom my soul loves: I sought him, and I did not find.

15. Quaesivi, et non inveni illum; vocavi, et non respondit mihi. (SS.5:6)
    I sought, and I did not find him; I called, and he did not respond to me.

16. Non enim veni vocare justos sed peccatores. (Mt.9:13)
    For I have not come to call the just but sinners.

17. Deposuit potentes de sede et exaltavit humiles. (Lk.1:52)
    He has put down the powerful down from the seat and has exalted the humble.

18. Sicut dilexit me Pater, et ego dilexi vos. Manete in dilectione mea. (Jn.15:9)
    As the Father has loved me, I also have loved y'all. Remain in my love.

19. Respondit Thomas, et dixit ei: Dominus meus et Deus meus. Dixit ei Jesus: Quia vidisti me, Thoma, credidisti: beati qui non viderunt, et crediderunt. (Jn.20:28-29)
    Thomas responded and said to him, 'My Lord and my God.' Jesus said to him, 'Because you have seen me, Thomas, you have believed. Blessed are those who have not seen and have believed.'

20. Quod oculus non vidit, nec auris audivit, nec in cor hominis ascendit, quae praeparavit Deus iis qui diligunt illum. (1Cor.2:9)
That which the eye has not seen, nor the ear heard, nor ascended into the heart of a human, those things which God has prepared to those who love him.

21. Caritas ex Deo est. Et omnis qui diligit, ex Deo natus est, et cognoscit Deum. Qui non diligit, non novit Deum: quoniam Deus caritas est. (1Jn.4:7-8)
Love is out of God. And everyone who loves, is born out of God and recognizes God. He who does not love, has not known God, because God is love.

22. Adjutorium nostrum in nomine Domini. Qui fecit caelum et terram. (at Mass)
Our help is in the name of the Lord, who made heaven and earth.

23. Et salutare tuum da nobis. (at Mass)
And give your salvation to us.

24. Alma Redemptoris Mater... tu quae genuisti, natura mirante, tuum sanctum Genitorem... peccatorum miserere. (Advent Antiphon)
Kind Mother of the Redeemer, you who gave birth, with nature marveling, to your holy Creator, have mercy on sinners.

25. Attende Domine, et miserere, quia peccavimus tibi. (Lent Antiphon)
Attend, O Lord, and have mercy, because we have sinned to you.

26. Panem de caelo praestitisti eis, omne delectamentum in se habentem. (Benediction)
You have bestowed bread down from heaven to them, having in itself every delight.

27. Nisi credideritis, non intelligetis. (Augustine)
Unless you will have believed, you will not understand.

28. Sero te amavi, pulchritudo tam antiqua et tam nova. (Augustine)
Late have I loved you, O beauty so ancient and so new!

29. Hodie aperuit nobis clausa porta quod serpens in muliere suffocavit, unde lucet in aurora flos de Virgine Maria. (Hildegard)
Today the closed gate which the serpent suffocated in the woman has opened to us, whence the flower down from the Virgin Mary shines in the dawn.

30. Tu candidum lilium quod Deus ante omnem creaturam inspexit. (Hildegard)
You are a pure white lily which God looked into before every creature.

31. Dator salutis, Christus filius Dei, mundum salvavit per crucem et sanguinem. (Sechnall)
    The giver of salvation, Christ the Son of God, has saved the world through the Cross and Blood.

32. Vere benedicta tu in mulieribus, quoniam Evae maledictionem in benedictionem commutasti. (Sophronius of Jerusalem)
    Truly you are blessed among women, because you have changed the curse of Eve into a blessing.

33. O filii et filiae, Rex caelestis, Rex gloriae, morte surrexit hodie. (Tisserand)
    O sons and daughters, the heavenly King, the King of glory, has risen with (from) death today.

34. Veni, vidi, vici. (Caesar)
    I came, I saw, I conquered.

35. Nil sine magno vita labore dedit mortalibus. (Horace)
    Life has given nothing to mortals without great labor.

36. Quos amor verus tenuit tenebit. (Seneca)
    Those whom true love has held, it will hold.

37. Labor omnia vicit. (Virgil)
    Labor has conquered all things.

38. Ego autem rogavi pro te (episcopal motto)
    I, however, have asked for you.

39. In Deo speravi non timebo (episcopal motto)
    In God I have hoped; I will not fear.

40. Infirma mundi elegit Deus. (motto of Vital-Justin Grandin)
    God has chosen the infirm things of the world.

41. Fui quod es, eris quod sum. (commonly on tombstones)
    I have been that which you are; you will be that which I am.

42. Quod natura dedit, tollere nemo potest. (Latin Proverb)
    That which nature has given, no one is able to take away.

43. Adoramus te, Christe, et benedicimus tibi; quia per sanctam Crucem tuam redemisti mundi. (Alphonsus Liguori, *Way of the Cross*)
    We adore you, O Christ, and we bless you; because through your holy Cross you have redeemed the world.

44. O adorande Jesu, non Pilatus sed iniqua mea vita te ad mortem condemnavit. (Alphonsus Liguori, *Way of the Cross*)
    O Jesus to be adored, not Pilate but my unjust life has condemned you towards death.

45. Elegit eam Deus, et praeelegit eam. In tabernaculo suo habitare fecit eam. (*Little Office of the Immaculate Conception*)
    God chose her and pre-chose her. He made her to dwell in his own tabernacle.

46. Genuisti qui te fecit, et in aeternum permanes virgo. (Novena to the Blessed Virgin)
    You gave birth to him who made you, and you remain a virgin into eternity.

47. Quando cor nostrum visitas, tunc lucet ei veritas. (Bernard, *Jesu Dulcis Memoria*)
    When you visit our heart, then truth shines to it.

48. Veni, Creator Spiritus, mentes tuorum visita, imple superna gratia, quae tu creasti pectora. (Rabanus Maurus, *Veni Creator Spiritus*)
    Come, O Creator Spirit, visit the minds of your [people], fill the chests which you have created with heavenly grace.

49. Veni veni Adonai, qui populo in Sinai, legem dedisti vertice, in majestate gloriae. (*Veni Veni Emmanuel*)
    Come, come, O Lord, you who gave to the people on the peak of Sinai a law, in the majesty of glory.

50. Christus innocens Patri reconciliavit peccatores. (Wipo of Burgundy, *Victimae Paschali*)
    Christ, the innocent one to the Father, has reconciled sinners.

51. Dic nobis, Maria, quid vidisti in via? Sepulcrum Christi viventis et gloriam vidi resurgentis. (Wipo of Burgundy, *Victimae Paschali*)
    Say to us, Mary: what have you seen on the way? I have seen the sepulcher of the living Christ and the glory of the rising one.

52. Magnificat anima mea Dominum, et exsultavit spiritus meus in Deo salvatore meo, quia respexit humilitatem ancillae suae. Ecce enim ex hoc beatam me dicent omnes generationes, quia fecit mihi magna, qui potens est, et sanctum nomen ejus… (Vespers Antiphon, Lk.1:46-49)
    My soul magnifies the Lord, and my spirit has exalted in God my savior, because he has looked back on the humility of his own maid-servant; for behold, all generations will say me to be blessed out of this, because he who is powerful has done great things to me, and his name is holy.

53. Nunc dimittis servum tuum, Domine, secundum verbum tuum in pace. Quia viderunt oculi mei salutare tuum quod parasti ante faciem omnium populorum: lumen ad revelationem gentium et gloriam plebis tuae Israel. (Compline Antiphon, Lk.2:29-32)
Now you send away your servant, Lord, according to your word in peace. Because my eyes have seen your salvation which you have prepared before the face of all peoples: a light towards the revelation of the nations and the glory of your common people Israel.

54. Salve, mundi Domina, caelorum Regina. Salve, Virgo virginum, stella matutina. Salve, plena gratia, clara luce divina. Mundi in auxilium, Domina, festina. Ab aeterno Dominus te praeordinavit matrem unigeniti Verbi, quo creavit terram, pontum, aethera, te pulchram ornavit sibi Sponsam, quae in Adam non peccavit. (*Little Office of the Immaculate Conception*)
Hello, Lady of the world, Queen of the heavens. Hello, Virgin of virgins, the early-morning star. Hello, full with grace, clear with divine light. Hurry into the help of the world, O Lady. From eternity the Lord preordained you to be mother of the only-begotten Word, with whom he created the earth, the sea, the sky; he adorned you to be a beautiful spouse to himself, who sinned not in Adam.

Chapter Seventeen

1. Formavit igitur Dominus Deus hominem de limo terrae, et inspiravit in faciem ejus spiraculum vitae, et factus est homo in animam viventem. (Gen.2:7)
Therefore the Lord God formed a human down from the dirt of the earth, and he breathed into his face the breath of life, and the human was made into a living soul.

2. Propterea exaudivit Deus, et attendit voci deprecationis meae. (Ps.65:19)
Therefore God has heard, and he attended to the voice of my prayer.

3. Vulnerasti cor meum, soror mea, sponsa; vulnerasti cor meum in uno oculorum tuorum. (SS.4:9)
You have wounded my heart, my sister, spouse; you have wounded my heart in one of your eyes.

4. Multi autem sunt vocati pauci vero electi. (Mt.22:14)
However many are called, truly few are chosen.

5. Omni autem cui multum datum est, multum quaeretur ab eo. (Lk.12:48)
However to everyone to whom much has been given, much will be sought from him.

6. Et Verbum caro factum est, et habitavit in nobis: et vidimus gloriam ejus. (Jn.1:14)
And the Word has been made flesh and has dwelt in us: and we saw his glory.

7. Gratia et veritas per Jesum Christum facta est. (Jn.1:17)
   Grace and truth has been made through Jesus Christ.

8. Quod scripsi, scripsi. (Jn.19:21-22)
   That which I have written, I have written.

9. Conversi estis ad Deum a simulacris servire Deo vivo et vero. (1Thes.1:9)
   Y'all have been converted towards God from idols to serve the living and true God.

10. Et qui non inventus est in libro vitae scriptus, missus est in stagnum ignis. (Rev.20:15)
    And he who is not found written in the book of life, is sent into the lake of fire.

11. Et dixit mihi: Factum est: ego sum alpha et omega, initium et finis. Ego sitienti dabo de fonte aquae vitae, gratis. (Rev.21:6)
    And he said to me: It has been done. I am the alpha and the omega, the beginning and the end. I will give to the one thirsting down from the fountain of the water of life, freely.

12. Ecce Agnus Dei, ecce qui tollit peccata mundi. Beati qui ad cenam Agni vocati sunt. (at Mass)
    Behold the Lamb of God, behold he who takes away the sins of the world. Blessed are they who have been called towards the supper of the Lamb.

13. Ecce completa sunt omnia, quae dicta sunt per Angelum de Virgine Maria. (Advent Antiphon)
    Behold all things have been completed which have been said through the angel about the Virgin Mary.

14. O certe necessarium Adae peccatum, quod Christi morte deletum est. (Exsultet)
    O certain, necessary sin of Adam, which has been deleted by the death of Christ.

15. Et vere bene doctus est qui Dei voluntatem facit et suam voluntatem relinquit. (a Kempis)
    And truly he has been taught well who does the will of God and relinquishes his own will.

16. In omnibus requiem quaesivi, et nusquam inveni nisi in angulo cum libro. (a Kempis)
    I have sought rest in all things, and nowhere have I found [it] except in a corner with a book.

17. Sancti venite, Christi corpus sumite, sanctum bibentes, quo redempti sanguinem. (Sechnall)
    O saints, come, receive the body of Christ, drinking the holy blood by which you have been redeemed.

18. Alea jacta est. (Caesar)
    The die has been thrown.

19. Verba volant, scripta manent. (Caius Titus)
    Words fly, things written remain.

20. Fortibus est fortuna viris data. (Ennius)
    Fortune is given to strong men.

21. Ignis aurum probat, miseria fortes viros. (Seneca)
    Fire proves gold, misery strong men.

22. Amor meus crucifixus est (episcopal motto)
    My love has been crucified.

23. Assumpta est Maria (episcopal motto)
    Mary has been assumed.

24. Salve, pretiose sanguis, de vulneribus crucifixi Domini nostri Jesu Christi profluens! (Catholic Prayer)
    Hello, O precious blood, flowing forth down from the wounds of our Lord Jesus Christ crucified.

25. Nos quoque, qui sancto tuo redempti sumus sanguine... (*Christe Redemptor Omnium*)
    We also, who have been redeemed by your holy blood...

26. Hi diligentes invicem in Jesu amorem confluunt. (Leo XIII, *O Gente Felix Hospita*)
    These, loving one another, flow together into the love of Jesus.

27. Quando venit ergo sacri plenitudo temporis, missus est ab arce patris natus orbis conditor. (Venantius Fortunatus, *Pange Lingua*)
    When therefore the fullness of sacred time came, the Builder of the world was sent, born, from the fortress of the Father.

Chapter Eighteen

1. Non habebis deos alienos in conspectu meo. (Dt.5:7)
   You shall not have foreign gods in my sight.

2. Auditu auris audivi te: nunc autem oculus meus videt te. (Job.42:5)
   With the hearing of the ear I heard you, however now my eye sees you.

3. Gloria et divitiae in domo ejus, et justitia ejus manet in saeculum saeculi. (Ps.111:3)
   Glory and riches are in his house, and his justice remains into the age of age.

4. Justitia ejus manet in saeculum saeculi: cornu ejus exaltabitur in gloria. (Ps.111:9)
   His justice remains into the age of age: his horn will be exalted in glory.

5. Propter domum Domini Dei nostri quaesivi bona tibi. (Ps.121:9)
   Because of the house of the Lord our God I have sought good things to you.

6. Ecce nunc benedicite Dominum, omnes servi Domini: qui statis in domo Domini, in atriis domus Dei nostri. In noctibus extollite manus vestras in sancta, et benedicite Dominum. (Ps.133:1-2)
   Behold, now bless the Lord, all you servants of the Lord, who stand in the house of the Lord, in the courts of the house of our God. In the nights take up your hands into the holy places and bless the Lord.

7. Benedictus Dominus Deus meus, qui docet manus meas ad proelium, et digitos meos ad bellum. (Ps.143:1)
   Blessed be the Lord my God, who teaches my hands towards battle and my fingers towards war.

8. Vidi cuncta quae fiunt sub sole, et ecce universa vanitas et afflictio spiritus. (Ecc.1:14)
   I have seen all things which happen under the sun, and behold, it is all vanity and affliction of spirit.

9. Sapientia hominis lucet in vultu ejus. (Ecc.8:1)
   The wisdom of a human shines in his face.

10. Sanctus, sanctus, sanctus Dominus, Deus exercituum; plena est omnis terra gloria ejus. (Isa.6:3)
    Holy, holy, holy Lord, God of armies; all the earth is full with his glory.

11. Benedicite, omnes spiritus Dei, Domino: laudate et superexaltate eum in saecula. (Dan.3:65)
    Bless the Lord, all you spirits of God: praise and highly exalt him into the ages.

12. Benedicite, spiritus et animae justorum, Domino: laudate et superexaltate eum in saecula. (Dan.3:86)
    Bless the Lord, O spirits and souls of the just: praise and highly exalt him into the ages.

13. Erexit cornu salutis nobis, in domo David pueri sui. (Lk.1:69)
    He has raised the horn of salvation to us in the house of David his boy.

14. Palpate et videte, quia spiritus carnem et ossa non habet, sicut me videtis habere. (Lk.24:39)
    Lightly touch and see, because a spirit does not have flesh and bones like y'all see me to have.

15. Pater diligit Filium et omnia dedit in manu ejus. (Jn.3:35)
    The Father loves the Son and has given all things in his hand.

16. Dabit enim tibi Dominus in omnibus intellectum. (2Tim.2:7)
    For the Lord will give to you understanding in all things.

17. Et in hoc scimus quoniam manet in nobis, de Spiritu quem dedit nobis. (1Jn.3:24)
    And in this we know that he remains in us, down from the Spirit which he gave to us.

18. In nomine Patris, et Filii, et Spiritus Sancti. Dominus vobiscum. Et cum spiritu tuo. (at Mass)
    In the name of the Father, and of the Son, and of the Holy Spirit. The Lord be with y'all. And with your spirit.

19. Gloria Patri et Filio et Spiritui Sancto, sicut erat in principio et nunc et semper, et in saecula saeculorum. (Christian Doxology)
    Glory to the Father, and to the Son, and to the Holy Spirit, as it was in the beginning and now and always and into the ages of ages.

20. O Adonai, et Dux domus Israel, qui Moysi in igne flammae rubi apparuisti, et ei in Sina legem dedisti: veni ad redimendum nos in brachio extento. (Advent Antiphon)
    O Lord and leader of the house of Israel, you who appeared to Moses in the fire of the flame of the bush and gave to him on Sinai the law, come in order to redeem us in (with) an arm having been extended.

21. O Clavis David, et sceptrum domus Israel; qui aperis et nemo claudit; claudis, et nemo aperit: veni, et educ vinctum de domo carceris, sedentem in tenebris, et umbra mortis. (Advent Antiphon)
    O Key of David and scepter of the house of Israel, you who open and no one shuts, you who shut and no one opens, come and lead out the one having been chained down from the house of prison, sitting in the shadows and the shadow of death.

22. Vicit Leo de tribu Juda, Radix David, alleluia! (Anthony of Padua)
    The lion about the tribe of Judah, the root of David, has conquered, alleluia!

23. O spiraculum sanctitatis, O ignis caritatis, O dulcis gustus in pectoribus! (Hildegard)
    O breath of sanctity, O fire of charity, O sweet taste in the chests!

24. Diligam te, Domine, fortitudo mea, firmamentum meum, refugium meum, liberator meus, Deus meus, adjutor meus, protector meus, cornu salutis meae, et susceptor meus. (Hugo of St. Victor)
I will love you, Lord, my strength, my firmament, my refuge, my liberator, my God, my helper, my protector, the horn of my salvation, and my supporter.

25. Manum misi in ignem. (Jerome)
I have sent the hand into the fire.

26. Crede mihi, sacra populi lingua est. (Seneca the Elder)
Believe me, the tongue of the people is sacred.

27. Aperi eis Spiritus Christi (episcopal motto)
Open to them, O Spirit of Christ.

28. Spiritu ambulate (episcopal motto)
Walk with the Spirit.

29. Senatus Populusque Romanus (motto of Ancient Rome)
The Senate and Roman people

30. In nomine Patris et Filii et Spiritus Sancti. Amen. (Sign of the Cross)
In the name of the Father and of the Son and of the Holy Spirit. Amen.

31. Pange lingua gloriosi corporis mysterium, sanguinisque pretiosi, quem in mundi pretium fructus ventris generosi rex effudit gentium. (Aquinas, *Pange Lingua*)
Sing, O tongue, the mystery of the glorious body and precious blood which the king of the nations, the fruit of the generous womb, has poured out into [as] the price of the world.

32. Accende lumen sensibus, infunde amorem cordibus. (Rabanus Maurus, *Veni Creator Spiritus*)
Kindle light to the senses, pour in love to hearts.

33. Paradisi clavis et janua, fac nos duci quo, Mater, gloria coronaris. (Simon Stock, *Flos Carmeli*)
O key and door of Paradise, make us to be led by whom, Mother, you are crowned with glory.

34. Veni O Jesse Virgula, ex hostis tuos ungula, de specu tuos tartari, educ et antro barathri. (*Veni Veni Emmanuel*)
Come, O rod of Jesse, lead out your [people] out of the hoof of the enemy, down from the cave of hell, and the cavern of the abyss.

35. Benedictus es, Domine Deus Israel patris nostri, ab aeterno in aeternum. Tua est, Domine, magnificentia, et potentia, et gloria, atque victoria: et tibi laus: cuncta enim quae in caelo sunt et in terra, tua sunt: tuum, Domine, regnum, et tu es super omnes principes. Tuae divitiae, et tua est gloria: tu dominaris omnium. In manu tua virtus et potentia: in manu tua magnitudo, et imperium omnium. (1Chr.29:10-12)
Blessed are you, O Lord God of Israel our father, from eternity into eternity. Yours, O Lord, is the magnificence and the power and the glory and the victory, and to you is praise. For all things which are in heaven and on earth are yours. Yours, O Lord, is the kingdom, and you are over all princes. Riches are yours, and glory is yours. You govern all things. In your hand are virtue and power, in your hand is greatness and imperial power of all things.

Chapter Nineteen

1. Sed et Seth natus est filius, quem vocavit Enos: iste coepit invocare nomen Domini. (Gen.4:26)
But also to Seth was born a son, whom he called Enos: this one began to invoke the name of the Lord.

2. Vere Dominus est in loco isto, et ego nesciebam… Non est hic aliud nisi domus Dei, et porta caeli. (Gen.28:16-17)
Truly the Lord is in this place, and I was not knowing it. This is not other except the house of God and the gate of heaven.

3. Scio quia omnia potes, et nulla te latet cogitatio. (Job.42:2)
I know that you are able [to do] all things, and no thought is hidden with (from) you.

4. Quis est iste rex gloriae? Dominus fortis et potens, Dominus potens in praelio. (Ps.23:8)
Who is this king of glory? The Lord strong and power, the Lord power in battle.

5. Dominus adjutor meus et protector meus; in ipso speravit cor meum, et adjutus sum. (Ps.27:7)
The Lord is my helper and my protector; in the same person my heart has hoped, and I have been helped.

6. Emitte lucem tuam et veritatem tuam: ipsa me deduxerunt et adduxerunt in montem sanctum tuum, et in tabernacula tua. (Ps.42:3, at Mass)
Send out your light and your truth. These same things have led me down and led me forth into your holy mountain, and into your tabernacles.

7. Quoniam hic est Deus, Deus noster in aeternum, et in saeculum saeculi: ipse reget nos in saecula. (Ps.47:15)
That this is God, our God into eternity and into the age of age: the same will rule us into the ages.

8. Veritas mea et misericordia mea cum ipso: et in nomine meo exaltabitur cornu ejus. (Ps.88:25)
   My truth and my mercy are with the same, and in my name his horn will be exalted.

9. Quid est quod fuit? Ipsum quod futurum est. Quid est quod factum est? Ipsum quod faciendum est. Nihil sub sole novum. (Ecc.1:9-10)
   What is that which has been? The same thing which is about to be. What is that which has been done? The same thing which is about to be done. There is nothing new under the sun.

10. Tota pulchra es, amica mea. (SS.4:7)
    You are all beautiful, my girlfriend.

11. Qui timetis Dominum, credite illi… Qui timetis Dominum, sperate in illum… Qui timetis Dominum, diligite illum. (Sir.2:8-10)
    Y'all who fear the Lord, believe that one. Y'all who fear the Lord, hope in that one. Y'all who fear the Lord, love that one.

12. Magnificavit ergo Dominus Salomonem super omnem Israel: et dedit illi gloriam regni, qualem nullus habuit ante eum rex Israel. (1Chr.29:25)
    Therefore the Lord made Solomon great over all Israel, and he gave to that one the glory of the kingdom as no king of Israel had before him.

13. Beati pauperes spiritu: quoniam ipsorum est regnum caelorum. (Mt.5:3)
    Blessed are the poor with (regards to) spirit, because of the same people is the kingdom of the heavens.

14. Quicumque enim fecerit voluntatem Patris mei, qui in caelis est, ipse meus frater, et soror, et mater est. (Mt.12:50)
    For whosoever will have done the will of my Father, who is in the heavens, the same is my brother and my sister and my mother.

15. Qui enim fecerit voluntatem Dei, hic frater meus, et soror mea, et mater est. (Mk.3:35)
    For he who will have done the will of God, this is my brother and my sister and my mother.

16. Sumite, hoc est corpus meum. (Mk.14:22)
    Take, this is my body.

17. Hoc facite in meam commemorationem. (Mk.22:19, at Mass)
    Do this into my commemoration.

18. In mundo erat, et mundus per ipsum factus est, et mundus eum non cognovit. (Jn.1:10)
    He was in the world and the world was made through the same, and the world did not recognize him.

19. Ille erat lucerna ardens et lucens. (Jn.5:35 about John the Baptist)
    That one was a lamp, burning and shining.

20. In hoc cognovimus caritatem Dei, quoniam ille animam suam pro nobis posuit: et nos debemus pro fratribus animas ponere. (1Jn.3:16)
    In this we have known the love of God, because he put his soul (i.e. laid down his life) for us, and we ought to put [our] souls for [our] brothers.

21. Qui vicerit, possidebit haec: et ero illi Deus, et ille erit mihi filius. (Rev.21:7)
    He who will have conquered will possess these things: and I will be God to him, and he will be a son to me.

22. Suscipe, sancte Pater omnipotens aeterne Deus, hanc immaculatam hostiam. (at Mass)
    Receive, O holy Father almighty eternal God, this immaculate host.

23. Hoc est enim corpus meum. (at Mass)
    For this is my body.

24. Per ipsum, et cum ipso, et in ipso, est tibi Deo Patri omnipotenti, in unitate Spiritus Sancti, omnis honor et gloria, per omnia saecula saeculorum. Amen. (at Mass)
    Through the same and with the same and in the same, to you Father God almighty in the unity of the Holy Spirit, is all honor and glory through all ages of ages. Amen.

25. Fac me humilem et patientem in laboribus hujus vitae. (Alphonsus Liguori)
    Make me humble and patient in the labors of this life.

26. O bonitas infinita! O caritas infinita! Deus mihi se totum dedit, factus est totus meus! (Alphonsus Liguori)
    O infinite goodness, O infinite love! God has given all himself to me; he has been made all mine.

27. Tu solus, Deus meus, tu solus, solus es, et semper eris amor meus et omnia. (Alphonsus Liguori)
    You alone, O my God, you alone, you alone are and always will be my love and all things.

28. Hominem unius libri timeo. (Aquinas)
    I fear a human of one book.

29. Omne quod movetur, ab alio movetur. (Aquinas)
    Everything which is moved, is moved by another.

30. Unde per caritatem homo in Deo ponitur et cum eo unum efficitur. (Aquinas)
    Whence a human through love is put in God and made one with him.

31. Deum et animam scire cupio, nihil aliud. (Augustine)
    I desire to know God and the soul, nothing other.

32. Extra Ecclesiam nulla salus. (Cyprian)
    There is no salvation outside the Church.

33. Dilige illum, dilige te propter illum, dilige dona illius propter illum... Dilige in donis illius, quod data sunt ab illo. Illum tibi, et te illi dilige. (Hugo of St. Victor)
    Love him, love yourself because of him, love his gifts because of him, love in his gifts because they have been given from him. Love him to yourself and yourself to him.

34. Haec sunt verba tua, Christe, Veritas aeterna. (a Kempis)
    These are your words, O Christ, eternal truth.

35. O veritas Deus, fac me unum tecum in charitate perpetua. (a Kempis)
    O Truth, God, make me one with you in perpetual charity.

36. 'Regnum Dei intra vos est', dicit Dominus. Converte te ex toto corde tuo ad Dominum, et relinque hunc miserum mundum, et inveniet anima tua requiem. (a Kempis)
    The kingdom of God is within y'all, says the Lord. Convert yourself out of all your heart towards the Lord and relinquish this miserable world, and your soul will find rest.

37. Alpha et Omega, ipse Christus Dominus, venit venturus judicare homines. (Sechnall)
    The alpha and the omega, the same Christ the Lord, comes, about to come to judge humans.

38. Non sum uni angulo natus; patria mea totus hic est mundus. (Seneca)
    I am not born to one corner; my homeland is all this world.

39. Verus amicus… est enim is qui est tamquam alter idem. (Cicero)
    For a true friend is he who is just as another the same (i.e. as another self).

40. Disce, puer, virtutem ex me verumque laborem, fortunam ex aliis. (Virgil)
    Learn, boy, virtue and true labor out of me, fortune out of others.

41. Speravimus ista dum fortuna fuit. (Virgil)
    We have hoped these same things while there has been fortune.

42. O beata solitudo, O sola beatitudo! (Carthusian Motto)
    O blessed solitude, O only beatitudo!

43. Aliis non sibi clemens (episcopal motto)
    Clement to others, not to himself

44. Alter alterius onera portate (episcopal motto)
    Carry the works (burdens), one of another

45. Christo in aliis servire (episcopal motto)
    To serve Christ in others

46. Crux totius orbis lumen (episcopal motto)
    The Cross is the light of all the world.

47. Dominus ipse faciet (episcopal motto)
    The Lord himself will do [it].

48. Totus tuus (motto of John Paul the Great)
    All yours

49. Unus pro omnibus, omnes pro uno (motto of Switzerland)
    One for all, all for one

50. In hoc signo vinces. (seen by Constantine)
    In this sign you will conquer.

51. Quid haec ad aeternitatem? (Catholic phrase)
    What are these things towards eternity?

52. Aliud est dicere, aliud est facere. (Latin Proverb)
    It is another thing to say, it is another thing to do.

53. Nullus difficilis cupienti labor. (Latin Proverb)
    No labor is difficult to the one desiring.

54. In te credo, in te spero, te amo, te adoro, beata Trinitas unus Deus, miserere mei nunc et in hora mortis meae et salva me. Amen. (Catholic Prayer)
    I believe in you, I hope in you, I love you, I adore you, blessed Trinity one God: have mercy on me now and in the hour of my death and save me. Amen.

55. Pro dolorosa ejus passione, miserere nobis et totius mundi. (Divine Mercy Chaplet)
    For his sorrowful passion, have mercy on us and the whole world.

56. Ipse creavit illam in Spiritu Sancto, et effundit illam super omnia opera sua. (*Little Office of the Immaculate Conception*)
The same person created her in the Holy Spirit and poured her out over all his works.

57. Qui cuncta solus efficis, cunctisque solus sufficis, tu sola lux es omnibus, et praemium sperantibus. (*Aeterna Lux Divinitas*)
You who alone effect all things and alone suffice all things, are the only light to us and the reward to those hoping.

58. Jesu, Rex admirabilis et triumphator nobilis, dulcedo ineffabilis, totus desiderabilis! (Bernard, *Jesu Dulcis Memoria*)
O Jesus, admirable king and noble triumpher, ineffable sweetness, all desirable!

59. Te, Christe, solum novimus. (Prudentius, *Nox et Tenebrae*)
O Christ, we have known you alone.

60. In principio erat Verbum, et Verbum erat apud Deum, et Deus erat Verbum. Hoc erat in principio apud Deum. Omnia per ipsum facta sunt: et sine ipso factum est nihil quod factum est. In ipso vita erat, et vita erat lux hominum. Et lux in tenebris lucet, et tenebrae eam non comprehenderunt. (Jn.1:1-5)
In the beginning was the Word, and the Word was at God, and God was the Word. This was in the beginning at God. All things have been made through the same, and without the same nothing has been made which has been made. In the same was life, and life was the light of humans. And the light shines in the shadows, and the shadows have not comprehended it.

61. Nihil potest quietare voluntatem hominis, nisi bonum universale. Quod non invenitur in aliquo creato, sed solum in Deo, quia omnis creatura habet bonitatem participatam. Unde solus Deus voluntatem hominis implere potest. (Aquinas)
Nothing is able to quiet the will of a human except the universal good, which is not found in anything created but only in God, because every creature has goodness participated. Whence only God is able to fill the will of a human.

62. Suscipe, Domine, universam meam libertatem. Accipe memoriam, intellectum atque voluntatem omnem. Quidquid habeo vel possideo mihi largitus es; id tibi totum restituo. (Ignatius of Loyola)
Receive, O Lord, all my freedom. Accept the memory, understanding, and all the will. Whatever I have or possess you have granted to me; I restore it all to you.

Chapter Twenty

1. Appellavitque lucem Diem, et tenebras Noctem: factumque est vespere et mane, dies unus. (Gen.1:5)
   And he named the light 'Day' and the shadows 'Night:' and evening has been made and morning, one day.

2. Tecum principium in die virtutis tuae in splendoribus sanctorum. (Ps.109:5)
   With you is the beginning in the day of your virtue in the splendors of the holy ones.

3. Spes ejus in Domino Deo ipsius, qui fecit caelum et terram, mare, et omnia quae in eis sunt. (Ps.145:5-6)
   His hope is in the Lord his God, who made heaven and earth, the sea, and all things which are in them.

4. Cor gaudens exhilarat faciem. (Prv.15:13)
   A rejoicing heart exhilarates the face.

5. Benedicite, noctes et dies, Domino: laudate et superexaltate eum in saecula. (Dan.3:71)
   Bless the Lord, nights and days: praise and highly exalt him into the ages.

6. Qui manducat meam carnem et bibit meum sanguinem, in me manet, et ego in illo. (Jn.6:57)
   He who chews my flesh and drinks my blood remains in me and I in him.

7. Spe gaudentes. (Rom.12:12)
   Rejoicing with hope.

8. Et omnis qui habet hanc spem in eo, sanctificat se, sicut et ille sanctus est. (1Jn.3:3)
   And everyone who has this hope in him sanctifies himself as he also is holy.

9. Laudabo te semper omnibus diebus vitae meae. (Prayer of Manasseh)
   I will praise you always all the days of my life.

10. Hic est enim calix sanguinis mei novi et aeterni testamenti, mysterium fidei, qui pro vobis et pro multis effundetur in remissionem peccatorum. (at Mass)
    For this is the chalice of my blood, of the new and eternal testament, the mystery of faith, which for y'all and for many will be poured out into the remission of sins.

11. Tuis enim fidelibus, Domine, vita mutatur, non tollitur. (at Funeral Mass)
    For to your faithful, Lord, life is changed not taken away.

12. Haec nox est, de qua scriptum est: Et nox sicut dies illuminabitur. (Exsultet)
    This is the night about which it has been written: and the night will be illuminated like the day.

13. At sanguis tuus, O Jesu, spes mea est. Numquam, spero, te amare cessabo. (Alphonsus Liguori)
    But you blood, O Jesus, is my hope. Never, I hope, will I cease to love you.

14. Peccatores in re, sancti in se. (Augustine)
    Sinners in a thing, saints in themselves.

15. Amicitia quae desinere potest vera numquam fuit. (Jerome)
    Friendship which is able to cease was never true.

16. Hic autem in Sacramento altaris totus praesens es Deus meus, homo Christus Jesus. (a Kempis)
    However here in the Sacrament of the altar you are all present, my God, the human Christ Jesus.

17. Ratio humana debilis est, et falli potest; fides autem vera falli non potest. (a Kempis)
    Human reason is weak and is able to be deceived; however, true faith is not able to be deceived.

18. Omnium rerum principia parva sunt. (Cicero)
    The beginnings of all things are small.

19. Veritatem dies aperit. (Seneca)
    The day opens the truth.

20. Felix qui potuit rerum cognoscere causas. (Virgil)
    Happy is he who has been able to know the causes of things.

21. Ardente fide (episcopal motto)
    With burning faith

22. Caritate Christi fidelitate Mariae (episcopal motto)
    With the love of Christ, with the fidelity of Mary

23. Fides quaerens intellectum (motto of Anselm)
    Faith seeking understanding

24. Pro fide, lege, et rege (motto of Polish-Lithuanian Commonwealth)
    For faith, law, and king

25. Semper fidelis (motto of US Marine Corps)
    Always faithful

26. Spe Salvi (encyclical of Benedict XVI)
    Saved by hope

27. Sensus fidelium (Catholic phrase)
    Sense of the faithful

28. Fides et Ratio (encyclical of John Paul the Great)
    Faith and Reason

29. Gaudium et Spes (Vatican II document)
    Joy and Hope

30. Dum anima est, spes est. (Latin Proverb)
    While there is a soul, there is hope.

31. Tota voluntatis meae inclinatione ad te solum convertar, qui meo nimis dignus es amore. (Alphonsus Liguori, *Way of the Cross*)
    With all the inclination of my will I am converted towards you alone, who are excessively worthy with (regards to) my love.

32. Veni, Sancte Spiritus, reple tuorum corda fidelium, et tui amoris in eis ignem accende. (Catholic Prayer)
    Come, Holy Spirit, fill again the hearts of your faithful, and kindle in them the fire of your love.

33. Qui finis et exordium rerumque fons es omnium, tu solus es solacium, tu certa spes credentium. (*Aeterna Lux Divinitas*)
    You who are the end and beginning and fountain of all things, you alone are solace, you are the certain hope of those believing.

34. Aeterne rerum conditor, noctem diemque qui regis, et temporum das tempora! (Ambrose, *Aeterne Rerum Conditor*)
    O eternal Creator of things, you who rule the night and day and give the times of times.

35. In cruce latebat sola Deitas, at hic latet simul et Humanitas, ambo tamen credens atque confitens, peto quod petivit latro poenitens. (Aquinas, *Adoro Te Devote*)
    On the Cross was being hidden only Deity, but here is hidden at the same time also humanity, nevertheless both believing and confessing, I seek that which the repenting thief sought.

36. Panis angelicus fit panis hominum; dat panis coelicus figuris terminum. O res mirabilis! Manducat Dominum pauper servus et humilis. (Aquinas, *Panis Angelicus*)
    Angelic bread becomes the bread of humans; heavenly bread gives an end to figures. O marvelous thing! A poor and humble servant eats the Lord.

37. Christe qui splendor et dies, noctis tenebras detegis. (*Christe qui Splendor et Dies*)
    O Christ, you who are splendor and day, take off the shadows of night.

38. O majestas infinita, amor noster, spes, et vita: fac nos dignos te videre, tecum semper permanere. (*De Amore Jesu*)
    O infinite majesty, our love, hope, and life: make us worthy to see you, to remain with you always.

39. Dies irae, dies illa solvet saeclum in favilla, teste David cum Sibylla. (*Dies Irae*)
    Day of anger, that day will release the age in ash, with the witness of David with the Sibyl.

40. Lacrimosa dies illa, qua resurget ex favilla, judicandus homo reus. (*Dies Irae*)
    That tearful day, on which guilty man about to be judged will arise out of the ash.

41. Qui Mariam absolvisti, et latronem exaudisti, mihi quoque spem dedisti. (*Dies Irae*)
    You who absolved Mary and heard the thief have also given hope to me.

42. Primo dierum omnium, quo mundus exstat conditus vel quo resurgens conditor nos, morte victa, liberat. (Gregory the Great, *Primo Dierum Omnium*)
    On the first of all days, on which the world stands out having been built or on which the builder, rising, with death conquered, frees us.

43. Veni Clavis Davidica, regna reclude caelica, fac iter tutum superum, et claude vias inferum. (*Veni Veni Emmanuel*)
    Come, Davidic Key, reveal the heavenly kingdoms, make safe the journey to the upper (places) and shut the ways to hell.

44. O crux ave spes unica, hoc passionis tempore, auge piis justitiam, reisque dona veniam. (Venantius Fortunatus, *Vexilla Regis*)
    Hail O Cross the only hope! In this time of passion, enlarge justice to the pious and grant pardon to the guilty.

45. Surrexit Christus spes mea. (Wipo of Burgundy, *Victimae Paschali*)
    Christ my hope has arisen.

46. Non sum ego Christus: sed quia missus sum ante illum. Qui habet sponsam, sponsus est: amicus autem sponsi, qui stat, et audit eum, gaudio gaudet propter vocem sponsi. Hoc ergo gaudium meum impletum est. (Jn.3:28-29)
I am not the Christ, but that I have been sent before him. He who has the bride is the bridegroom; the friend of the bridegroom, however, who stands and listens to him, rejoices with joy because of the voice of the bridegroom. Therefore this my joy has been filled.

47. Salve Regina, Mater misericordiae, vita, dulcedo, et spes nostra salve. Ad te clamamus exsules filii Hevae, ad te suspiramus, gementes et flentes in hac lacrimarum valle. Eia ergo, advocata nostra, illos tuos misericordes oculos ad nos converte; et Jesum, benedictum fructum ventris tui, nobis post hoc exsilium ostende. O clemens, O pia, O dulcis Virgo Maria. (Hermann of Reichenau)
Hello Queen, Mother of mercy, our life, sweetness, and hope: hello. Towards you we call, exiles, sons of Eve; towards you we sigh, groaning and weeping in this valley of tears. O therefore, our advocate, turn towards us those your merciful eyes and show to us after this exile Jesus, the blessed fruit of your womb. O clement, O pious, O sweet Virgin Mary!

Chapter Twenty-one

1. Parce mihi, nihil enim sunt dies mei. (Job.7:16)
Spare me, for nothing are my days.

2. Scio enim quod redemptor meus vivit, et in novissimo die de terra surrecturus sum… et in carne mea videbo Deum meum. (Job.19:25-26)
For I know that my redeemer lives, and on the newest day I am going to be raised up from the earth, and in my flesh I will see my God.

3. Melius est nomen bonum quam unguenta pretiosa, et dies mortis die nativitatis. (Ecc.7:2)
A good name is better than precious ointment, and the day of death than the day of birth.

4. Melior est finis orationis quam principium. (Ecc.7:9)
The end of a speech is better than the beginning.

5. Melior est patiens arrogante. (Ecc.7:9)
The patient one is better than the arrogant one.

6. Melior est canis vivus leone mortuo. (Ecc.9:4)
A living dog is better than a dead lion.

7. Dicite Deo: Quam terribilia sunt opera tua, Domine! (Ps.65:3)
Say to God: How terrible are your works, Lord!

8. Timor Domini delectabit cor. (Sir.1:12)
   The fear of the Lord will delight the heart.

9. Et Filius Altissimi vocabitur, et dabit illi Dominus Deus sedem David patris ejus: et regnabit in domo Jacob in aeternum. (Lk.1:32-33)
   And he will be called Son of the Highest, and the Lord God will give to him the seat of David his father, and he will reign in the house of Jacob into eternity.

10. Carissimi, non mandatum novum scribo vobis, sed mandatum vetus, quod habuistis ab initio. Mandatum vetus est verbum, quod audistis. (1Jn.2:7)
    Dearest ones, I write to y'all not a new command but an old command which you have had from the beginning. The old command is the word which you have heard.

11. In hoc cognoscitur Spiritus Dei: omnis spiritus qui confitetur Jesum Christum in carne venisse, ex Deo est. (1Jn.4:2)
    In this is the Spirit of God recognized: every spirit which confesses Jesus Christ to have come in the flesh is out of God.

12. Et dixit qui sedebat in throno: Ecce nova facio omnia. Et dixit mihi: Scribe, quia haec verba fidelissima sunt, et vera. (Rev.21:5)
    And he who was sitting on the throne said, 'Behold, I make all things new.' And he said to me, 'Write, because these words are most faithful and true.'

13. Te igitur, clementissime Pater, per Jesum Christum, Filium tuum, Dominum nostrum, supplices rogamus ac petimus. (at Mass)
    Therefore, O most clement Father, through Jesus Christ your Son our Lord, we, kneeling, ask and seek you.

14. O Mater alma Christi carissima, suscipe pia laudum praeconia. (Adrian Fortescue)
    O dearest kind Mother of Christ, receive the pious proclamations of praises.

15. Sequentia de Sancto Michaele, quam Alcuinus composuit Karolo imperatori. Summi regis archangele Michahel, intende quaesumus nostris vocibus. (Alcuin)
    The sequence about Saint Michael, which Alcuin composed to the emperor Charles. O highest of the king, O archangel Michael: focus, we seek, to our voices.

16. Audi nos, Michahel, angele summe. (Alcuin)
    Hear us, O Michael, highest angel.

17. Parce mihi, o Bonitas infinita, per amorem Jesu Christi, quia te offendisse toto corde me paenitet. (Alphonsus Liguori)
    Spare me, O infinite goodness, through the love of Jesus Christ, because I repent with all [my] heart to have offended you.

18. Melior est in via, amor Dei quam Dei cognitio. (Aquinas)
    Love of God is better on the way than thought of God.

19. Summe, optime, potentissime, omnipotentissime, misericordissime et justissime, secretissime et praesentissime, pulcherrime et fortissime, stabilis et incomprehensibilis, immutabilis mutans omnia, numquam novus numquam vetus, innovans omnia. (Augustine)
    Highest, best, most powerful, most omnipotent, most merciful and most just, most secret and most present, most beautiful and most strong, stable and incomprehensible, unchanging, changing all, never new, never old, innovating all things.

20. Aliquid amplius invenies in silvis quam in libris. (Bernard)
    You will find anything more in the forests than in books.

21. Ecce deus fortior me! (Dante)
    Behold, a god stronger than me!

22. Adoramus te, sanctissime Domine Jesu Christe, hic et ad omnes ecclesias tuas, quae sunt in toto mundo, et benedicimus tibi; quia per sanctam Crucem tuam redemisti mundum. Amen. (Francis of Assisi)
    We adore you, most holy Lord Jesus Christ, here and towards all your churches which are in all the world, and we bless you: because through your holy Cross you have redeemed the world. Amen.

23. Lucis Creator optime! (Gregory the Great)
    O best Creator of light!

24. Praesta Pater piissime! (Gregory the Great)
    O most pious Father, bestow!

25. O pulcherrima et dulcissima, quam valde Deus in te delectabatur! (Hildegard about the Virgin Mary)
    O most beautiful and sweet, how God was being very delighted in you!

26. Audivi enim saepe, securius esse audire et accipere consilium quam dare. (a Kempis)
    For I have often heard that it is more secure to hear and to receive counsel than to give.

27. Humilis tui cognitio certior via est ad Deum, quam profundae scientiae inquisitio. (a Kempis)
    A humble thought of yours is a more certain way towards God than the investigation of profound science.

28. Multos in summa pericula misit venturi timor ipse mali. (Lucan)
    The fear of a bad thing about to come itself has sent many into the highest dangers.

29. Brevissima ad divitias per contemptum divitiarum via est. (Seneca)
    The shortest way towards riches is through the contempt of riches.

30. Maximum remedium irae mora est. (Seneca)
    The greatest remedy of anger is delay.

31. Pejor est bello timor ipse belli. (Seneca)
    The fear itself of war is worse than war.

32. Pax optima rerum. (Silius Italicus)
    Peace is the best of things.

33. Ad majorem dilectionem (episcopal motto)
    Towards a greater love

34. Carior libertas (episcopal motto)
    Freedom is more dear.

35. Caritas major autem (episcopal motto)
    However charity is greater.

36. Delectabor in Domino (episcopal motto)
    I will be delighted in the Lord.

37. Dulcius melle fortius leone (episcopal motto)
    Sweeter than honey, stronger than a lion

38. Tu summum bonum es (episcopal motto)
    You are the highest good thing.

39. Ad majorem Dei gloriam (motto of Jesuits)
    Towards the greater glory of God

40. Virtus unita fortior. (motto of Andorra)
    Virtue is stronger united.

41. Excelsior (motto of New York)
    Higher

42. Esse quam videri (motto of North Carolina)
    To be than to be seen

43. Sapientia melior auro. (motto of the University of Deusto)
    Wisdom is better than gold.

44. E pluribus unum (motto of USA)
    Out of many, one

45. Vetus Testamentum (Christian phrase)
    The Old Testament

46. Summa Theologiae (title of Aquinas' masterpiece)
    The highest things of theology

47. Pater aeterne, offero tibi corpus et sanguinem, animam et divinitatem dilectissimi Filii tui, Domini nostri, Jesu Christi, in propitiatione pro peccatis nostris et totius mundi. (Divine Mercy Chaplet)
    Eternal Father, I offer to you the body and blood, soul and divinity, of your most beloved Son, our Lord, Jesus Christ, in atonement for our sins and of the whole world.

48. O quam suavis est Domine spiritus tuus. (*Little Office of the Blessed Sacrament*)
    O how sweet is your spirit, O Lord!

49. Civitas altissimi, porta orientalis: in te est omnis gratia, Virgo singularis. (*Little Office of the Immaculate Conception*)
    City of the Highest, gate of the eastern thing (i.e. the sun): in you is every grace, O singular Virgin.

50. Ego in altissimis habito, et thronus meus in columna nubis. (*Little Office of the Immaculate Conception*)
    I dwell in the highest places and my throne is in a column of cloud.

51. O Victima caritatis, Cor amantissimum Jesu, pro peccatis nostris immolatum, ab ingratis hominibus neglectum et afflictum, converte nos, vivifica nos, accende nos. (*Little Office of the Sacred Heart of Jesus*)
    O victim of love, most loving heart of Jesus, sacrificed for our sins, neglected and afflicted by ungrateful humans, convert us, make us alive, kindle us.

52. O sacrum Cor Jesu, salutis nostrae sitientissimum! (Sacred Heart Novena)
    O sacred heart of Jesus, most thirsting of our salvation!

53. Visus, tactus, gustus, in te fallitur; sed auditu solo tuto creditur. Credo quidquid dixit Dei Filius; nil hoc verbo veritatis verius. (Aquinas, *Adoro Te Devote*)
    Sight, touch, taste is deceived in you; but by hearing alone does one believe safely. I believe whatever the Son of God has said; nothing is more true than this word of truth. (This is an exceptionally difficult passage. 'Visus, tactus, gustus' are fourth declension nouns derived from the perfect passive participle and 'tuto' is an adverb derived from the ablative of the adjective 'tutus'.)

54. Jesu spes paenitentibus, quam pius es petentibus! Quam bonus te quaerentibus, sed quid invenientibus? (Bernard, *Jesu Dulcis Memoria*)
    O Jesus, hope to those repenting, how pious you are to those seeking! How good to those seeking you, but what to those finding?

55. Caeli Deus sanctissime! *(Caeli Deus Sanctissime)*
    O most holy God of heaven!

56. O Sanctissima, O Piissima, dulcis virgo Maria! (*O Sanctissima*)
    O most holy, O most pious, sweet Virgin Mary!

57. Scimus Christum surrexisse a mortuis vere: tu nobis, victor Rex, miserere. (Wipo of Burgundy, *Victimae Paschali*)
    We know Christ to have risen truly from the dead: you, have mercy on us, victor king.

58. O ineffabilis decor Dei excelsi et purissima claritas lucis aeternae, vita omnem vitam vivificans, lux omne lumen illuminans et conservans in splendore perpetuo multiformia lumina fulgentia, ante thronum divinitatis tuae a primaevo diluculo! (Bonaventure)
    O ineffable glory of God Most High and purest clarity of eternal light, life making every life alive, light illuminating every light and conserving in perpetual splendor many-formed glistening lights, before the throne of your divinity from the primeval dawn!

59. Benedictus Deus. Benedictum Nomen Sanctum ejus. Benedictus Jesus Christus, verus Deus et verus homo. Benedictum Nomen Jesu. Benedictum Cor ejus sacratissimum. Benedictus Sanguis ejus pretiosissimus. Benedictus Jesus in sanctissimo altaris Sacramento. Benedictus Sanctus Spiritus, Paraclitus. Benedicta excelsa Mater Christi, Maria sanctissima. Benedicta sancta ejus et Immaculata Conceptio. Benedicta ejus gloriosa Assumptio. Benedictum nomen Mariae, Virginis et Matris. Benedictus sanctus Joseph, ejus castissimus Sponsus. Benedictus Deus in Angelis suis, et in Sanctis suis. Amen. (The Divine Praises)
    Blessed be God. Blessed be his holy name. Blessed be Jesus Christ, true God and true human. Blessed be the name of Jesus. Blessed be his most sacred heart. Blessed be his most precious blood. Blessed be Jesus in the most holy Sacrament of the altar. Blessed be the Holy Spirit, the Paraclete. Blessed be the highest Mother of Christ, Mary most holy. Blessed be her holy and immaculate conception. Blessed be her glorious assumption. Blessed be the name of Mary, virgin and mother. Blessed be

Saint Joseph, her most chaste spouse. Blessed be God in his angels and in his saints. Amen.

Chapter Twenty-two

1. Dixitque Deus: 'Fiat lux.' Et facta est lux. (Gen.1:3)
   And God said, 'Let light become.' And light was made.

2. Convertat Dominus vultum suum ad te, et det tibi pacem. (Num.6:24-26)
   May the Lord turn his face towards you and give to you peace.

3. Sit nomen Domini benedictum ex hoc nunc et usque in saeculum. (Ps.112:2)
   May the name of the Lord be blessed out of this, now, and all the way into the age.

4. Fiat pax in virtute tua: et abundantia in turribus tuis. (Ps.121:7)
   Let peace happen in your virtue, and abundance in your towers.

5. Melius est videre quod cupias, quam desiderare quod nescias. Sed et hoc vanitas est, et praesumptio spiritus. (Ecc.6:9)
   It is better to see that which you might desire than to desire that which you might not know. But this also is vanity and presumption of spirit.

6. Non est enim homo justus in terra qui faciat bonum et non peccet. (Ecc.7:21)
   For there is not a just human on earth who might do good and not sin.

7. Benedicat terra Dominum: laudet et superexaltet eum in saecula. (Dan.3:74)
   Let the earth bless the Lord: let it praise and highly exalt him into the ages.

8. Benedicat Israel Dominum: laudet et superexaltet eum in saecula. (Dan.3:83)
   Let Israel bless the Lord: let him praise and highly exalt him into the ages.

9. Ecce ego mittam vobis Eliam prophetam, antequam veniat dies Domini magnus et horribilis. Et convertet cor patrum ad filios, et cor filiorum ad patres eorum. (Mal.4:5-6)
   Behold, I will send to y'all Elijah the prophet before the day of the Lord should come, the great and horrible [day]. And may be converted the heart of fathers towards sons and the heart of sons towards their fathers.

10. Beati mundo corde: quoniam ipsi Deum videbunt. (Mt.5:8)
    Blessed are they with a clean heart: because the same will see God.

11. Dixit autem Maria: Ecce ancilla Domini: fiat mihi secundum verbum tuum. (Lk.1:38)
    However Mary said, 'Behold the maid-servant of the Lord: let it happen to me according to your word.'

12. Non diligamus verbo neque lingua, sed opere et veritate. (1Jn.3:18)
    We should not love with word nor tongue but with deed and truth.

13. Carissimi, diligamus nos invicem. (1Jn.4:7)
    Dearest ones, let us love one another.

14. Et clamor meus ad te veniat. (at Mass)
    And may my shout come towards you.

15. Oremus. (at Mass)
    Let us pray.

16. Gratias agamus Domino Deo nostro. (at Mass)
    Let us give thanks to the Lord our God.

17. Suscipiat Dominus sacrificium de manibus tuis, ad laudem et gloriam nominis sui, ad utilitatem quoque nostram, totiusque Ecclesiae suae sanctae. (at Mass)
    May the Lord receive the sacrifice down from your hands towards the praise and glory of his name, also towards our utility and of all his holy Church.

18. Benedicas haec dona, haec munera, haec sancta sacrificia. (at Mass)
    May you bless these gifts, these services, these holy sacrifices.

19. Pax Domini sit semper vobiscum. (at Mass)
    May the peace of the Lord be always with you.

20. Corpus/Sanguis Domini nostri Jesu Christi custodiat animam meam in vitam aeternam. (at Mass)
    May the body/blood of our Lord Jesus Christ guard my soul into eternal life.

21. Benedicat vos omnipotens Deus, Pater, et Filius, et Spiritus Sanctus. (at Mass)
    May almighty God bless y'all: Father, and Son, and Holy Spirit.

22. Benedicamus Domino. (at the Divine Office)
    Let us bless the Lord.

23. Divinum Auxilium maneat semper nobiscum. (at the Divine Office)
    May the Divine help remain always with us.

24. Requiescant in pace. (at the Divine Office)
    May they rest in peace.

25. Adoremus in aeternum sanctissimum Sacramentum. (Eucharistic Antiphon)
    Let us adore into the eternal, most holy Sacrament.

26. Ave, ave, ave, coeli panis vive. Laudetur in aeternum sanctissimum Sacramentum. (Eucharistic Antiphon)
Hail, hail, hail, alive bread of heaven. May he be praised into the eternal, most holy Sacrament.

27. In paradisum deducant te angeli; in tuo adventu suscipiant te martyres, et perducant te in civitatem sanctam Jerusalem. Chorus angelorum te suscipiat, et cum Lazaro quondam paupere aeternam habeas requiem. (Funeral Antiphon)
May angels lead you down into paradise; may the martyrs receive you in your arrival and may they lead you through into the holy city Jerusalem. May a chorus of angels receive you, and, with Lazarus the former poor man, may you have eternal rest.

28. Requiem aeternam dona eis Domine, et lux perpetua luceat eis. (Funeral Antiphon)
Eternal rest grant to them, O Lord, and let perpetual light shine to them.

29. Gloria, laus et honor tibi sit, Rex Christe, Redemptor: cui puerile decus prompsit Hosanna pium. (Palm Sunday Antiphon)
May glory, praise, and honor be to you, King Christ Redeemer, to whom a boyish honor prompted a pious Hosanna.

30. Sed nihil possum, nisi tu adjuves me gratia tua. (Alphonsus Liguori)
But I am able [to do] nothing unless you should help me with your grace.

31. Delectet me, Domine, labor qui est pro te. (Aquinas)
O Lord, may the labor which is for you delight me.

32. Omne verum, a quocumque dicatur, a Spiritu Sancto est. (Aquinas)
Every true thing, from whomever it may be said, is from the Holy Spirit.

33. Et quis locus est in me quo veniat in me Deus meus, quo Deus veniat in me, Deus qui fecit caelum et terram? (Augustine)
And what is the place in me where my God might come into me, where God might come into me, the God who made heaven and earth?

34. Fecisti nos ad te et inquietum est cor nostrum donec requiescat in te. (Augustine)
You have made us towards yourself and inquiet is our heart until it should rest in you.

35. Spes nostra non sit, nisi in Deo. (Augustine)
May our hope not be except in God.

36. Operi Dei nihil praeponatur. (Benedict)
Let nothing be put before the work of God.

37. Et ideo mens nostra tantis splendoribus irradiata et superfusa, nisi sit caeca, manu duci potest per semetipsam ad contemplandam illam lucem aeternam. (Bonaventure)
    And therefore our mind, illuminated and endowed with so great splendors, unless it should be blind, is able to be led by the hand through itself in order to contemplate that eternal light.

38. Oro, Domine, intellectum illumines, voluntatem inflammes, cor emundes, animam sanctifices. (Clement XI)
    I pray, O Lord: may you illumine the understanding, may you inflame the will, may you clean out the heart, may you sanctify the soul.

39. Spiritui Sancto honor sit. (Hildegard)
    May honor be to the Holy Spirit.

40. Ratio ducat, non fortuna. (Livy)
    Let reason lead, not fortune.

41. Vive cum hominibus tamquam deus videat. (Seneca)
    Live with humans just as [if] god should see.

42. Igitur qui desiderat pacem, praeparet bellum. (Vegetius)
    Therefore he who desires peace should prepare war.

43. Quis fallere possit amantem? (Virgil)
    Who might be able to deceive one loving?

44. Absit gloriari nisi in Cruce Domini nostri Jesu Christi (episcopal motto)
    May it be away to be gloried except in the Cross of our Lord Jesus Christ.

45. Adveniat regnum tuum (episcopal motto)
    Let your kingdom come.

46. Ametur cor Jesu (episcopal motto)
    May the heart of Jesus be loved.

47. Christi simus non nostri (episcopal motto)
    May we be of Christ and not of ourselves.

48. Deus det nobis pacem (episcopal motto)
    May God give to us peace.

49. Crux sancta sit mihi lux. (initialled on the medal of St. Benedict)
    May the holy Cross be a light to me.

50. Tu Mater viventium et porta es sanctorum, nova stella Jacob, Domina angelorum... Porta et refugium sis Christianorum. (*Little Office of the Immaculate Conception*)
You are Mother of the living and gate of the saints, the new star of Jacob, the Lady of angels; may you be a gate and refuge of Christians.

51. Genitori Genitoque laus et jubilatio, salus, honor, virtus quoque sit et benedictio. (Aquinas, *Pange Lingua*)
To the begetter and to the begotten be praise, jubilation, salvation, honor, virtue also and benediction.

52. Sis, Jesu, nostrum gaudium, qui es futurus praemium: sit nostra in te gloria, per cuncta semper saecula. (Bernard, *Jesu Dulcis Memoria*)
O Jesus, may you be our joy, you who are a reward about to come; may our glory be in you through all the ages always.

53. Sit Christe Rex piissime, tibi Patrique gloria, cum Spiritu Paraclito, in sempiterna saecula. (*Christe qui Splendor et Dies*)
O Christ, pious king, may glory be to you and to the Father, with the Spirit, the Paraclete, into everlasting ages.

54. Da pacem, Domine, in diebus nostris, quia non est alius qui pugnet pro nobis nisi tu Deus noster. (*Da Pacem Domine*)
Give peace, O Lord, in our days, because there is not another who might fight for us except you our God.

55. Jubilemus et cantemus in beata coeli vita. Amen! Jesu fiat ita. (*De Amore Jesu*)
Let us jubilate and sing in the blessed life of heaven. Amen! So may it happen, O Jesus!

56. Deo Patri sit gloria, ejusque soli Filio, cum Spiritu Paraclito, nunc et per omne saeculum. (*Jam Lucis Orto Sidere*)
May glory be to God the Father and to his only Son, with the Spirit the Paraclete, now and through every age.

57. Jesu, tibi sit gloria, qui natus es de Virgine, cum Patre, et almo Spiritu, in sempiterna saecula. (*Jam Morte Victor Obruta*)
O Jesus, may glory be to you, you who were born down from the Virgin, with the Father and the kind Spirit, into everlasting ages.

58. Audit tyrannus anxius adesse regum principem, qui nomen Israel regat teneatque David regiam. (Prudentius, *Cathemerinon*)
The anxious tyrant hears the prince of kings to be present, who might rule the name of Israel and hold the royal house of David.

59. Christum canamus Principem, natum Maria Virgine. (Sedulius, *A Solis Ortus*)
    Let us sing about Christ the Prince, born [from] the Virgin Mary.

60. Benedicamus Patrem, et Filium cum Sancto Spiritu. Laudemus et superexaltemus eum in saecula. (*Trisagium Angelicum*)
    Let us bless the Father and the Son with the Holy Spirit. Let us praise and highly exalt him into the ages.

61. Victimae paschali laudes immolent Christiani. (Wipo of Burgundy, *Victimae Paschali*)
    May Christians sacrifice (offer) praises of the paschal victim.

62. Visita, quaesumus, Domine, habitationem istam, et omnes insidias inimici ab ea longe repelle: Angeli tui sancti habitent in ea, qui nos in pace custodiant, et benedictio tua sit super nos semper, per Christum Dominum nostrum. Amen. (Compline Prayer)
    Visit, we seek, O Lord, this dwelling, and all snares of the enemy repel far from it. May your holy angels dwell in it, who might guard us in peace, and may your blessing be over us always through Christ our Lord. Amen.

63. Dic nunc, totum 'cor meum', dic nunc Deo: 'Quaero vultum tuum, vultum tuum, Domine, requiro.' Eia nunc ergo tu, Domine Deus meus, doce cor meum ubi et quomodo quaerat ubi et quomodo te inveniat. (Anselm quoting Ps.26)
    Say, now, all my heart, say now to God: 'I seek your face, your face, O Lord, I require.' O now therefore you, O Lord my God: teach my heart where and how it might seek, where and how it might find you.

64. Ave, crux sancta, virtus nostra. Ave, crux adoranda, laus et gloria nostra. Ave, crux, auxilium et refugium nostrum. Ave, crux, consolatio omnium moerentium. Salve, crux, victoria et spes nostra. Salve, crux, defensio et vita nostra. Salve, crux, redemptio et liberatio nostra. Salve, crux, signum salutis, atque inexpugnabilis murus contra omnem virtutem inimici. Sit mihi crux semper spes Christianitatis meae. Sit mihi crux resurrectio mortis meae. Sit mihi crux triumphus adversus daemones. Sit mihi crux mater consolationis meae. (Anselm)
    Hail, holy Cross, our virtue. Hail, Cross to be adored, our praise and glory. Hail, Cross, our help and refuge. Hail, Cross, consolation of all those mourning. Hello, Cross, our victory and hope. Hello, Cross, our defense and life. Hello, Cross, our redemption and liberation. Hello, Cross, sign of salvation and unconquerable wall against all the virtue of the enemy. May the Cross always be to me the hope of my Christianity. May the Cross be to me the resurrection of my death. May the Cross be to me a triumph against demons. May the Cross be to me the mother of my consolation.

65. Adeste fideles, laeti triumphantes, Venite venite in Bethlehem, Natum videte, Regem Angelorum. Deum de Deo, lumen de lumine, Gestant puellae viscera, Deum verum, genitum non factum. Cantet nunc io, chorus angelorum, Cantet nunc aula caelestium. Gloria gloria, in excelsis Deo. Ergo qui natus, die hodierna, Jesu tibi sit gloria. Patris aeterni, Verbum caro factum. Venite adoremus, venite adoremus, venite adoremus Dominum. (Christmas Carol)
Be present, O faithful ones, happy, triumphing ones: come, come into Bethlehem, see the one born king of angels. The inner organs of the girl bear God from God, light from light, true God begotten not made. Now may a chorus of angels sing, 'Hooray.' Now may the royal court of the heavenly places sing: 'Glory, glory to God in the highests.' Therefore, O Jesus who have been born today, to you be glory. The Word of the eternal Father has been made flesh. Come, let us adore; come, let us adore; come, let us adore the Lord.

Chapter Twenty-Three

1. Observa diem sabbati, ut sanctifices eum, sicut praecepit tibi Dominus Deus tuus. (Dt.5:12)
   Observe the day of the Sabbath in order that you might sanctify it, as the Lord your God commanded you.

2. Ventus est vita mea, et non revertetur oculus meus ut videat bona. (Job.7:7)
   My life is wind, and my eye will not be turned back in order that it might see good things.

3. In te, Domine, speravi; non confundar in aeternum. (Ps.30:2)
   In you, O Lord, I have hoped; may I not be confounded into eternity.

4. Angelis suis mandavit de te, ut custodiant te in omnibus viis tuis. (Ps.90:11)
   He has commanded his angels about you, in order that they may guard you in all your ways.

5. Benedicat tibi Dominus ex Sion, et videas bona Jerusalem omnibus diebus vitae tuae, et videas filios filiorum tuorum: pacem super Israel. (Ps.127:5-6)
   May the Lord bless you out of Zion, and may you see the good things of Jerusalem all the days of your life, and may you see the sons of your sons, peace be over Israel.

6. Audi, fili mi, disciplinam patris tui, et ne dimittas legem matris tuae. (Prv.1:8)
   Hear, my son, the discipline of your father, and may you not send away the law of your mother.

7. Sic luceat lux vestra coram hominibus: ut videant opera vestra bona, et glorificent Patrem vestrum, qui in caelis est. (Mt.5:16)
   Thus may your light shine before humans: so that they might see your good deeds and glorify your Father who is in the heavens.

8. Et ait angelus ei: Ne timeas, Maria: invenisti enim gratiam apud Deum. (Lk.1:30)
   And the angel says to her, 'Do not fear, Mary: for you have found grace at God.'

9. Qui autem facit veritatem, venit ad lucem, ut manifestentur opera ejus, quia in Deo sunt facta. (Jn.3:21)
   However he who does the truth, comes towards the light so that his deeds might be manifested that they have been done in God.

10. Ego lux in mundum veni, ut omnis qui credit in me, in tenebris non maneat. (Jn.12:46)
    I came as light into the world, so that everyone who believes in me might not remain in the shadows.

11. Hoc est praeceptum meum, ut diligatis invicem sicut dilexi vos. (Jn.15:12)
    This is my command, that y'all should love one another as I have loved y'all.

12. Haec mando vobis: ut diligatis invicem. (Jn.15:17)
    These things I command to y'all: that y'all should one another.

13. Haec est autem vita aeterna: ut cognoscant te, solum Deum verum, et quem misisti Jesum Christum. (Jn.17:3)
    These things, however, are eternal life: that they should recognize you, the only true God, and Jesus Christ whom you have sent.

14. Et sublevatis oculis in caelum, [Jesus] dixit: Pater, venit hora: clarifica Filium tuum, ut Filius tuus clarificet te. (Jn.17:1)
    And with eyes raised into the sky, Jesus said, 'Father, the hour has come: make your Son renowned so that your Son may make you renowned.'

15. Haec autem scripta sunt ut credatis, quia Jesus est Christus Filius Dei: et ut credentes, vitam habeatis in nomine ejus. (Jn.20:31)
    However these things have been written so that y'all might believe that Jesus is Christ, the Son of God, and so that believing y'all might have life in his name.

16. Infirma mundi elegit ut confundat fortia. (1Cor.1:27)
    He chose the infirm things of the world in order to confound the strong things.

17. Quoniam Filium suum unigenitum misit Deus in mundum, ut vivamus per eum. (1Jn.4:9)
    Because God has sent his only-begotten Son into the world that we might live through him.

18. Et hoc mandatum habemus a Deo: ut qui diligit Deum, diligat et fratrem suum. (1Jn.4:21)
    And we have this command from God: that he who loves God, should love also his brother.

19. Orate fratres ut meum ac vestrum sacrificium acceptabile fiat apud Deum Patrem omnipotentem. (at Mass)
    Pray, brothers, so that my and your sacrifice might become acceptable at God the Father almighty.

20. Domine, non sum dignus ut intres sub tectum meum, sed tantum dic verbo, et sanabitur anima mea. (at Mass)
    O Lord, I am not worthy that you should enter under my roof, but only say with the word and my soul will be healed.

21. Haec nox est, in qua, destructis vinculis mortis, Christus ab inferis victor ascendit. (Exsultet)
    This is the night on which, with the chains of death having been destroyed, Christ ascended from the underworld [as] the victor.

22. Suscipe me Domine secundum eloquium tuum et vivam, et non confundas me ab expectatione mea. (Monastic Consecration)
    Receive me, Lord, according to your word and I will live, and do not confound me from my expectation.

23. Amantissime Domine mi, doleo ex tota anima mea de peccatis meis. (Alphonsus Liguori)
    O my most loving Lord, I mourn out of all my soul about my sins.

24. Ne permittas, ne permittas me separari a te. (Alphonsus Liguori)
    May you not permit, may you not permit me to be separated from you.

25. Credo ut intelligam. (Augustine)
    I believe in order that I might understand.

26. Non enim amat Deus damnare sed salvare, et ideo patiens est in malos, ut de malis faciat bonos. (Augustine)
    For God does not love to damn but to save, and therefore he is patient into bad people, so that he might make good people down from bad people.

27. Rogamus te, Domine, ut sis adjutor et auxiliator noster. (Clement I)
    We ask you, Lord, that you might be our helper and helper.

28. Adoro te ut primum principium; desidero ut finem ultimum; laudo ut benefactorem perpetuum; invoco ut defensorem propitium. (Clement XI)
    I adore you as the first beginning; I desire [you] as the ultimate end; I praise [you] as the perpetual benefactor; I invoke [you] as the kind defender.

29. O splendidissima gemma... fons saliens de corde Patris! (Hildegard)
    O most splendid gem, fountain leaping down from the heart of the Father!

30. Quis ego sum ut praestes mihi temetipsum? (a Kempis)
    Who am I that you should bestow yourself to me?

31. Sed unde mihi hoc ut venias ad me? (a Kempis)
    But from where is this to me that you should come towards me?

32. Quis mihi det, Domine, ut inveniam te solum, ut aperiam tibi totum cor meum? (a Kempis)
    Who might give to me, Lord, in order that I might find you alone, in order that I might open all my heart to you?

33. Vivas ut possis. (Caecilius Statius)
    You should live as you might be able to.

34. Numquam enim temeritas cum sapientia commiscetur. (Cicero)
    For never is rashness mixed with wisdom.

35. Amor misceri cum timore non potest. (Publilius Syrus)
    Love is not able to be mixed with fear.

36. Ut in omnibus glorificetur Deus. (Benedictine motto, 1Pet.4:11)
    In order that in all things God might be glorified.

37. Ora et labora ut habeant vitam (episcopal motto)
    Pray and work in order that they might have life.

38. Do ut des. (Latin phrase)
    I give in order that you might give.

39. Ave, augustissima Regina pacis, sanctissima Mater Dei, per sacratissimum Cor Jesu Filii tui Principis pacis, fac ut quiescat ira ipsius et regnet super nos in pace. (Catholic Prayer)
    Hail, most august Queen of peace, most holy Mother of God, through the most sacred heart of Jesus your Son the Prince of Peace; make so that the same person's anger might be still and he might reign over us in peace.

40. O sacrum Cor Jesu, diligentibus te beneficentissimum, deficiat in te caro nostra et cor nostrum, ut sis amor cordis nostri et pars nostra in aeternum. (*Little Office of the Sacred Heart of Jesus*)
    O sacred heart of Jesus, most beneficent to those loving you, may our flesh and our heart fail in you so that you might be the love of our heart and our part into eternity.

41. Paratum cor meum, Deus cordis mei, ut faciam voluntatem tuam. (*Little Office of the Sacred Heart of Jesus*)
    My heart is prepared, O God of my heart, in order that I might do your will.

42. Sic fiat, ut nos caritas jungat. (Leo XIII, *O Gente Felix Hospita*)
    May it become thus, that charity might join us.

43. Veni O Sapientia, quae hic disponis omnia, veni viam prudentiae, ut doceas et gloriae. (*Veni Veni Emmanuel*)
    Come, O wisdom, you who arrange all things here; come in order that you might teach the way of prudence and glory.

44. Veni veni Rex gentium, veni Redemptor omnium, ut salves tuos famulos, peccati sibi conscios. (*Veni Veni Emmanuel*)
    Come, come, O King of the nations, come, O Redeemer of all, in order that you might save your servants, conscious to themselves of sin.

45. Domine Jesu Christe, qui dixisti: Petite et accipietis; quaerite et invenietis; pulsate et aperietur vobis; quaesumus, da nobis petentibus divinissimi tui amoris affectum, ut te toto corde, ore et opere diligamus et a tua numquam laude cessemus. (Sacred Heart Novena)
    O Lord Jesus Christ, who said, 'Ask and y'all will receive, seek and y'all will find, knock and it will be opened to y'all,' we seek, give to us asking the affection of your Divine love so that with all [our] heart, mouth, and deed we might love you and never cease from your praise.

46. Cur igitur non amem te, O Jesu amantissime, non ut in coelo salves me, aut ne aeternum damnes me, nec praemii ullius spe, sed sicut tu amasti me? Sic amo et amabo te, solum quia Rex meus es, et solum quia Deus es. (Francis Xavier, *O Deus Ego Amo Te*)
    Therefore, why should not love you, O most loving Jesus, not so that you might save me in heaven or that you might not damn me for eternity, nor with the hope of any reward, but as you have loved me? Thus I love and I will love you, only because you are my king, only because you are God.

47. Homo quidam fecit coenam magnam et misit servum suum hora coenae dicere invitatis, ut venirent: quia parata sunt omnia. Venite comedite panem meum et bibite vinum quod miscui vobis. Gloria Patri et Filio, et Spiritui Sancto. (Antiphon from the Octave of Corpus Christi)
    A certain human made a great dinner and sent his servant at the hour of dinner to say to the invited ones so that they would come, because all things have been prepared: Come, eat my bread and drink the wine which I have mixed to y'all. Glory to the Father and to the Son and to the Holy Spirit.

48. Pater noster, qui es in caelis: sanctificetur nomen tuum; adveniat regnum tuum; fiat voluntas tua, sicut in caelo et in terra. Panem nostrum cotidianum da nobis hodie; et dimitte nobis debita nostra, sicut et nos dimittimus debitoribus nostris; et ne nos inducas in tentationem; sed libera nos a malo. (The Lord's Prayer)
Our Father, who are in the heavens, may your name be sanctified. May your kingdom arrive, may your will happen, as in heaven and on earth. Give our daily bread to us today, and forgive us our debts, as we also forgive our debtors. And may you not lead us in into temptation, but free us from badness.

49. O Domina mea, sancta Maria, me in tuam benedictam fidem ac singularem custodiam et in sinum misericordiae tuae, hodie et quotidie et in hora exitus mei animam meam et corpus meum tibi commendo. Omnem spem et consolationem meam, omnes angustias et miserias meas, vitam et finem vitae meae tibi committo, ut per tuam sanctissimam intercessionem et per tua merita, omnia mea dirigantur et disponantur opera secundum tuam tuique Filii voluntatem. Amen. (Aloysius Gonzaga)
O my Lady, holy Mary, I will guard myself into your blessed and singular faith and into the bosom of your mercy, today and everyday, and in the hour of my exit I commend my soul and my body to you. My every hope and consolation, all my anguishes and miseries, life and the end of my life I commit to you so that through your most holy intercession and through your merits all my works may be guided and arranged according to your will and [the will] of your Son. Amen.

Chapter Twenty-four

1. Speret Israel in Domino ex hoc nunc et usque in saeculum. (Ps.130:3)
May Israel hope in the Lord, out of this now all the way into the age.

2. Haec dicit Dominus: State super vias, et videte, et interrogate de semitis antiquis quae sit via bona, et ambulate in ea: et invenietis refrigerium animabus vestris. Et dixerunt: Non ambulabimus. (Jer.6:16)
The Lord says these things: Stand over the ways and see, and interrogate about the ancient footpaths, which might be the good way, and walk in it, and y'all will find coolness to your souls. And they said, 'We will not walk.'

3. Hic est Filius meus dilectus in quo mihi complacui. (Mt.3:17)
This is my beloved Son in whom I have been pleased to myself.

4. Amen dico vobis, quicumque non acceperit regnum Dei sicut puer, non intrabit in illud. (Lk.18:17)
Amen I say to y'all, whosoever will have not accepted the kingdom of God like a boy will not enter into it.

5. Quodcumque dixerit vobis, facite. (Jn.2:5)
Whatsoever he may have said to y'all, do [it]!

6. Haec est autem voluntas Patris mei, qui misit me: ut omnis qui videt Filium et credit in eum, habeat vitam aeternam, et ego resuscitabo eum in novissimo die. (Jn.6:40)
   However, this is the will of my Father who sent me: that everyone who sees the Son and believes in him might have eternal life, and I will resuscitate him on the newest day.

7. Venit hora, ut clarificetur Filius hominis. (Jn.12:23)
   The hour has come that the Son of a human may be made renowned.

8. Et jam non sum in mundo, et hi in mundo sunt, et ego ad te venio. Pater sancte, serva eos in nomine tuo, quos dedisti mihi: ut sint unum, sicut et nos. (Jn.17:11)
   And now I am not in the world, and these are in the world, and I come towards you. Holy Father, preserve them, whom you gave to me, in your name: that they might be one as we also [are].

9. Placuit Deo… salvos facere credentes. (1Cor.1:21)
   It has been pleasing to God to make saved those believing.

10. Elegit nos… ut essemus sancti et immaculati in conspectu ejus. (Eph.1:4)
    He chose us in order that we might be holy and immaculate in his sight.

11. Haec est enim caritas Dei, ut mandata ejus custodiamus. (1Jn.5:3)
    For this is the love of God, that we might guard his commands.

12. In spiritu humilitatis, et in animo contrito suscipiamur a te, Domine: et sic fiat sacrificium nostrum in conspectu tuo hodie, ut placeat tibi, Domine Deus. (at Mass)
    In the spirit of humility, and in a contrite soul may we be received by you, Lord: and thus may our sacrifice become in your sight today so that it might be pleasing to you, O Lord God.

13. O inaestimabilis dilectio caritatis: ut servum redimeres, Filium tradidisti! (Exsultet)
    O inestimable love of charity: in order that you might redeem a slave you handed over the Son.

14. Libera me, Domine, de morte aeterna, in die illa tremenda, quando caeli movendi sunt et terra, dum veneris judicare saeculum per ignem. (Funeral Antiphon)
    Free me, Lord, down from eternal death, on that tremendous day when the heavens and the earth are about to be moved, while you would come to judge the age through fire.

15. Factus est Deus homo ut homo fieret Deus. (Augustine)
    God has been made a human in order that a human might become God.

16. Ille praedicat quantum erectus sit Christus a te: Christus autem dicit quantum descendit ad te. (Augustine)
He preaches how great Christ may have been raised from (above) you: Christ however says how great he has descended towards you.

17. Nondum amabam, et amare amabam...quaerebam quid amarem, amans amare. (Augustine)
I was not yet loving, and I was loving to love… I was seeking what I might love, loving to love.

18. Sed ego peccator eam mereri non possum. (Innocent III)
But I am a sinner, I am not able to merit it.

19. Hoc oro, hoc desidero, ut tibi totus uniar. (a Kempis)
This I pray, this I desire, that I might be made all one to (with) you.

20. Nescire autem quid antequam natus sis acciderit, id est semper esse puerum. (Cicero)
However to not know what may have happened before you were born, it is always to be a boy.

21. Sedit qui timuit ne non succederet. (Horace)
He sat who feared that he would not succeed.

22. Ne quid nimis. (Terence)
Do not [do] what [would be] too much.

23. Domine ut serviam (episcopal motto)
O Lord, that I might serve

24. Domine ut videam (episcopal motto)
O Lord, that I might see

25. Leo terram propriam protegat. (motto of South Georgia and the South Sandwich Islands)
The lion protects his own land.

26. Cor Jesu, o melle dulcius, puris amicum mentibus, puris amandum cordibus, in corde regnes omnium. (*Little Office of the Sacred Heart of Jesus*)
O heart of Jesus, O sweeter honey, friend to pure minds, to be loved by pure hearts, may you reign in the heart of all things.

27. O sacrum Cor Jesu, Patris voluntati obsequentissimum, inclina ad te corda nostra, ut quae placita sunt ei faciamus semper. (*Little Office of the Sacred Heart of Jesus*)
O sacred heart of Jesus, most submissive to the will of the Father, incline our hearts towards you in order that those things which have been pleasing to him we might always do.

28. Christusque nobis sit cibus, potusque noster sit fides. (Ambrose, *Splendor Paternae Gloriae*)
And may Christ be food to us, and may faith be our drink.

29. Jesu, quem velatum nunc aspicio, oro fiat illud quod tam sitio: ut te revelata cernens facie, visu sim beatus tuae gloriae. Amen. (Aquinas, *Adoro te Devote*)
O Jesus, whom I look at now veiled, I pray: may happen which I so thirst: that discerning you with revealed face, I might be blessed with the vision of your glory.

30. Uni trinoque Domino, sit sempiterna gloria, qui vitam sine termino, nobis donet in patria. (Aquinas, *O Salutaris Hostia*)
To the one and triple Lord be everlasting glory, who might grant to us life without end in homeland.

31. Sub tuum praesidium confugimus, sancta Dei Genitrix: nostras deprecationes ne despicias in necessitatibus: sed a periculis cunctis libera nos semper, Virgo gloriosa et benedicta. (Ancient Compline Antiphon)
We flee together underneath your protection, holy mother of God: may you not despise our prayers in necessities, but free us always from all dangers, O glorious and blessed Virgin. (sub followed by the accusative case indicates direction)

32. Non pro eis rogo tantum, sed et pro eis qui credituri sunt per verbum eorum in me: ut omnes unum sint, sicut tu Pater in me, et ego in te, ut et ipsi in nobis unum sint: ut credat mundus, quia tu me misisti. Et ego claritatem, quam dedisti mihi, dedi eis: ut sint unum, sicut et nos unum sumus. Ego in eis, et tu in me: ut sint consummati in unum: et cognoscat mundus quia tu me misisti, et dilexisti eos, sicut et me dilexisti. Pater, quos dedisti mihi, volo ut ubi sum ego, et illi sint mecum: ut videant claritatem meam, quam dedisti mihi: quia dilexisti me ante constitutionem mundi. (Jn.17:20-24)
Not for them only do I pray, but also for those who are going to believe in me through their word: that they all may be one, as you Father are in me, and I in you, that those same also might be one in us, in order that the world might believe that you have sent me. And I have given to them the renown which you gave to me: that they might be one, as we also are one. I in them and you in me: may they be consumed into one, and may the world recognize that you have sent me, and you have loved them as you have also loved me. Father, those whom you have given to me I want that where I am they may also be with me, in order that they may see my renown which you have given to me, because you have loved me before the arrangement of the world.

33. Anima Christi, sanctifica me. Corpus Christi, salva me. Sanguis Christi, inebria me. Aqua lateris Christi, lava me. Passio Christi, conforta me. O bone Jesu, exaudi me. Intra tua vulnera absconde me. Ne permittas me separari a te. Ab hoste maligno defende me. In hora mortis meae voca me, et jube me venire ad te, ut cum Sanctis tuis laudem te, in saecula saeculorum. Amen. (Catholic Prayer)
Soul of Christ, sanctify me. Body of Christ, save me. Blood of Christ, inebriate me. Water of the side of Christ, wash me. Passion of Christ, comfort me. O good Jesus, hear me. Within your wounds hide me. Do not permit me to be separated from you. From the malignant enemy defend me. In the hour of my death call me, and order me to come towards you, so that with your saints I might praise you into the ages of ages. Amen.

34. Salvum fac populum tuum, Domine, et benedic haereditati tuae. Et rege eos, et extolle illos usque in aeternum. Per singulos dies benedicimus te. Et laudamus nomen tuum in saeculum, et in saeculum saeculi. Dignare, Domine, die isto sine peccato nos custodire. Miserere nostri, Domine, miserere nostri. Fiat misericordia tua, Domine, super nos, quemadmodum speravimus in te. In te, Domine, speravi: non confundar in aeternum. (Te Deum addition)
Make saved your people, Lord, and bless your inheritance. And rule them, and take them out all the way into eternity. Through single days we bless you, and we praise your name into the age, and into the age of age. Deign, Lord, to guard us this day without sin. Have mercy on us, Lord, have mercy on us. Let your mercy, O Lord, happen over us, just as we have hoped in you. In you, Lord, I have hoped. May I not be confounded into eternity.

Chapter Twenty-five

1. Deus in domibus ejus cognoscetur cum suscipiet eam. (Ps.47:4)
God will be recognized in her homes when he will support her.

2. Ne dicas amico tuo: Vade, et revertere: cras dabo tibi: cum statim possis dare. (Prv.3:28)
Do not say to your friend: Go and turn back, tomorrow I will give to you, when you might be able to give immediately.

3. Cum ergo natus esset Jesus in Bethlehem Juda in diebus Herodis regis, ecce magi ab oriente venerunt Jerosolymam, dicentes: Ubi est qui natus est rex Judaeorum? Vidimus enim stellam ejus in oriente, et venimus adorare eum. (Mt.2:2)
Therefore when Jesus had been born in Bethlehem of Judah in the days of king Herod, behold, magi from the east came to Jerusalem saying: Where is he who has been born king of the Jews? For we saw his star in the east and have come to adore him.

4. Cum autem venerit Filius hominis in majestate sua, et omnes angeli cum eo, tunc sedebit super sedem majestatis suae. (Mt.25:31)
   However, when the Son of a human should have come in his majesty, and all the angels with him, then he will sit over the seat of his majesty.

5. Carissimi, nunc filii Dei sumus: et nondum apparuit quid erimus. Scimus quoniam cum apparuerit, similes ei erimus: quoniam videbimus eum sicuti est. (1Jn.3:2)
   Dearest ones, now we are sons of God: and not yet has it appeared what we will be. We know that when it should have appeared, we will be similar to him, because we will see him as he is.

6. O Jesu jucundissime, amabilis Jesu, o bone Jesu, exaudi me. O mater mea, et spes mea, Maria, tu quoque exaudi me et ora Jesum pro me. (Alphonsus Liguori)
   O most pleasant Jesus, lovable Jesus, O good Jesus, hear me. O my mother and my hope, Mary, you also hear me and pray (to) Jesus for me.

7. Christi corpus, ave, sancta de virgine natum, viva caro, Deitas integra, verus homo. Salve vera salus, vis, vita, redemptio mundi: liberet a cunctis nos tua dextera malis. (Anselm)
   Hail, body of Christ, born down from the holy virgin, alive flesh, integral Deity, true human. Hello true salvation, strength, life, redemption of the world: may your right hand free us from all bad things.

8. Numquam minus solus, quam cum solus. (John Henry Newman)
   Never less alone than when alone.

9. Nam cum Deus inspexit faciem hominis quem formavit, omnia opera sua in eadem forma hominis integra aspexit. (Hildegard)
   For when God inspected the face of the human whom he had formed, he looked at all his works in the same integral form of the human. (i.e. God sees the world in us)

10. Vi et armis. (Cicero)
    With strength and weapons.

11. Vi victa vis. (Cicero)
    Strength having conquered with strength

12. Qui terret plus ipse timet. (Claudian)
    He who terrifies, the same person fears more.

13. Ut desint vires, tamen est laudanda voluntas. (Ovid)
    That (Although) strengths might be lacking, nevertheless the will is to be praised.

14. Facilius est multa facere quam diu. (Quintilian)
    It is more doable (easier) to do many things than for a long time.

15. Non ille diu vixit, sed diu fuit. (Seneca)
    That one did not live for a long time, but he was for a long time.

16. Qui non vetat peccare cum possit, jubet. (Seneca)
    He who does not forbid to sin when he might be able to, orders [it].

17. Plura consilio quam vi perfecisse (Tacitus)
    To have perfected more things with counsel than with strength

18. Multis e gentibus vires (motto of Saskatchewan)
    Strengths out of many nations

19. Ex unitate vires (motto of South Africa)
    Strengths out of unity

20. Per veritatem vis. (motto of Washington University in St. Louis)
    Strength through truth

21. Contra vim mortis non crescit herba in hortis. (Medieval medicinary)
    Against the strength of death, an herb does not grow in the gardens.

22. Te mens adoret sobria ut cum profunda clauserit diem caligo noctium, fides tenebras nesciat et nox fide reluceat. (Ambrose, *Deus Creator Omnium*)
    Let a sober mind adore you so that, when the profound gloom of the nights should have closed the day, faith might not know the shadows, and the night might shine again with faith.

23. Eia Mater Domini, quae pacem reddidisti angelis et homini, cum Christum genuisti: tuum exora Filium ut se nobis propitium exhibeat et deleat peccata. (*Angelus ad Virginem*)
    O Mother of the Lord, you who gave back peace to angels and human(kind) when you gave birth to Christ, pray fervently to your Son so that he might exhibit himself favorable to us and delete sins.

24. Mors stupebit et natura, cum resurget creatura, Judicanti responsura. (*Dies Irae*)
    Death will be stunned, and nature (also), when the creature shall rise about to respond to the one judging.

25. Judex ergo cum sedebit, quidquid latet apparebit: nil inultum remanebit. (*Dies Irae*)
    Therefore when the Judge will sit, whatever is hidden will appear: nothing will remain unavenged.

26. O quam tristis et afflicta, fuit illa benedicta, mater unigeniti; quae maerebat et dolebat, et tremebat cum videbat, nati poenas inclyti. (*Stabat Mater Dolorosa*)
O how sad and afflicted was that blessed mother of the holy-begotten, who was lamenting and sorrowing and trembling when she was seeing the punishments of the famous one having been born.

27. Eia, Mater, fons amoris, me sentire vim ardoris fac, ut tecum sentiam. (*Stabat Mater Speciosa*)
O Mother, fountain of love, make me to sense the strength of ardor so that I might sense with you.

28. Audivit Jesus quia ejecerunt eum foras: et cum invenisset eum, dixit ei: Tu credis in Filium Dei? Respondit ille, et dixit: Quis est, Domine, ut credam in eum? Et dixit ei Jesus: Et vidisti eum, et qui loquitur tecum, ipse est. At ille ait: Credo, Domine. Et procidens adoravit eum. Et dixit Jesus: In judicium ego in hunc mundum veni: ut qui non vident videant, et qui vident caeci fiant. (Jn.9:35-39)
Jesus heard that they had cast him outside, and when he had found him, he said to him, 'Do you believe in the Son of God?' That one responded and said, 'Who is he, Lord, that I might believe in him?' And Jesus said to him, 'And you have seen him, and he who is speaking with you, the same is he. And that one says, 'I believe, Lord.' And falling forward, he adored him. And Jesus said, 'I came into this world into (for) judgment, so that they who do not see might see, and they who see might become blind.

29. Dicit Simoni Petro Jesus: Simon Joannis, diligis me plus his? Dicit ei: Etiam Domine, tu scis quia amo te. Dicit ei: Pasce agnos meos. Dicit ei iterum: Simon Joannis, diligis me? Ait illi: Etiam Domine, tu scis quia amo te. Dicit ei: Pasce agnos meos. Dicit ei tertio: Simon Joannis, amas me? (Jn.21:15-17)
Jesus says to Simon Peter, 'Simon of John, do you love me more than these?' He says to him, 'Also (yes), Lord, you know that I love you.' He says to him, 'Shepherd my lambs,' He says to him again, 'Simon of John, do you love me?' He says to that one, 'Also, Lord, you know that I love you.' He says to him, 'Shepherd my lambs.' He says to him a third time, 'Simon of John, do you love me?'

Chapter Twenty-six

1. Aufer iram a corde tuo. (Ecc.11:10)
Carry away anger from your heart.

2. In die illa dicetur Jerusalem: Noli timere, Sion. (Zeph.3:16)
On that day it will be said of Jerusalem, 'Do not fear, Zion.'

3. Ecce angelus Domini apparuit in somnis ei, dicens: Joseph, fili David, noli timere accipere Mariam conjugem tuam: quod enim in ea natum est, de Spiritu Sancto est. (Mt.1:20)
   Behold, the angel of the Lord appeared in dreams to him, saying, 'Joseph, Son of David, do not fear to receive Mary [to be] your spouse, for that which has been conceived in her is down from the Holy Spirit.

4. Nolite judicare, ut non judicemini. (Mt.7:1)
   Do not judge, so that y'all might not be judged.

5. Nolite dare sanctum canibus. (Mt.7:6)
   Do not give a holy thing to dogs.

6. Omnia ergo quaecumque vultis ut faciant vobis homines, et vos facite illis. Haec est enim lex, et prophetae. (Mt.7:12)
   Therefore all things whatsoever y'all want that humans should do to y'all, y'all also do to them. For this is the law and the prophets.

7. Et nolite timere eos qui occidunt corpus, animam autem non possunt occidere. (Mt.10:28)
   And do not fear those who kill the body, however are not able to kill the soul.

8. Qui enim habet, dabitur illi: et qui non habet, etiam quod habet auferetur ab eo. (Mk.4:25)
   For he who has, it will be given to that one, and he who does not have, also that which he has will be carried away from him.

9. Et respondens Jesus dixit illi: Quid tibi vis faciam? Caecus autem dixit ei: Rabboni, ut videam. (Mk.10:51)
   And Jesus, responding, said to that one, 'What do you want (that) I should do to you?' However, the blind man said to him, 'Teacher, that I might see.'

10. Stans autem Jesus jussit illum adduci ad se. Et cum appropinquasset, interrogavit illum, dicens: Quid tibi vis faciam? At ille dixit: Domine, ut videam. (Lk.18:40-41)
    Jesus, however, standing, ordered him to be led towards himself. And when he had approached, he interrogated him, saying, 'What do you want (that) I should do to you?' And he said, 'Lord, that I might see.'

11. Ille autem dicit eis: Ego sum, nolite timere. (Jn.6:20)
    However that one says to them, 'I am, do not fear.'

12. Etsi mihi non vultis credere, operibus credite, ut cognoscatis, et credatis quia Pater in me est, et ego in Patre. (Jn.10:38)
    Even if y'all do not want to believe me, believe the deeds, so that y'all might recognize and believe that the Father is in me and I am in the Father.

13. Dicebant ergo Pilato pontifices Judaeorum: Noli scribere: Rex Judaeorum: sed quia ipse dixit: Rex sum Judaeorum. Respondit Pilatus: Quod scripsi, scripsi. (Jn.19:21-22)
    Therefore the high priests of the Jews were saying to Pilate: Do not write, 'King of the Jews,' but that the same person said, 'I am the King of the Jews.' Pilate responded: That which I have written, I have written.

14. Noli timere… propter quod ego sum tecum. (Acts.18:9-10)
    Do not fear… on account of that I am with you.

15. Nolite diligere mundum, neque ea quae in mundo sunt. (1Jn.2:15)
    Do not love the world, nor those things which are in the world.

16. Et spiritus, et sponsa dicunt: Veni. Et qui audit, dicat: Veni. Et qui sitit, veniat: et qui vult, accipiat aquam vitae, gratis. (Rev.22:17)
    And the spirit and the spouse say, 'Come.' And he who hears, should say, 'Come.' And he who thirsts should come, and he who wants should receive the water of life, freely.

17. Amo te, Deus meus, teque semper diligere volo. (Alphonsus Liguori)
    I love you, my God, and I want always to love you.

18. Amo te, o summum Bonum meum; diligo te, o Bonitas infinita; amo te, Deus meus, qui es infinito amore dignus, et semper repetere volo in tempore et in aeternitate: amo te, amo te. (Alphonsus Liguori)
    I love you, O my highest good; I love you, O infinite goodness; I love you, my God, you who are worthy with infinite love, and I want to always seek again in time and in eternity: I love you, I love you.

19. Dic ergo mihi quid me vis facere, sum enim paratus ad omnia. (Alphonsus Liguori)
    Therefore say to me what you want me to do, for I am prepared towards all things.

20. Quis me separabit a caritate Christi? O Redemptor amabilis, et quem alium diligere volo, nisi te, qui es infinita bonitas et infinito amore dignus? Quid mihi est in caelo et a te quid volui super terram? Deus cordis mei, et pars mea Deus in aeternum. (Alphonsus Liguori)
    Who will separate me from the love of Christ? O lovable Redeemer, and whom other do I want to love except you, who are infinite goodness and worthy with infinite love? What is there to me in heaven and away from you what have I wanted over the earth? The God of my heart, and my part is God into eternity.

21. Deus... confer salutem corporum veramque pacem cordium. (Ambrose, *Rector Potens Verax Deus*)
O God, confer salvation of bodies and true peace of hearts.

22. Ama Deum et fac quid vis. (Augustine)
Love God and do what you want.

23. Jube quod vis. (Augustine)
Order what you want.

24. Et quod sibi quis fieri non vult, alio ne faciat. (Benedict)
And that which [any]one does not want to happen to himself, he should not do to another.

25. Offero tibi, Domine cogitanda, ut sint ad te; dicenda, ut sint de te; facienda, ut sint secundum te; ferenda, ut sint propter te. Volo quidquid vis, volo quia vis, volo quomodo vis, volo quamdiu vis. (Clement XI)
I offer to you, O Lord, those things about to be thought, that they might be towards you, those things about to be said, that they might be about you, those things about to be done, that they might be according to you, those things about to be carried, that they might be because of you. I want whatever you want, I want because you want, I want how you want, I want for how long you want.

26. Quare ergo, Deus meus, fecisti me, nisi quia esse magis quam non esse voluisti me? (Hugo of St. Victor)
Why, therfore, my God, did you make me, unless because you wanted me to be more than not to be.

27. Vis ut diligam te. (Hugo of St. Victor)
You want that I should love you.

28. Stude ergo cor tuum ab amore visibilium abstrahere, et ad invisiblia te transferre. (a Kempis)
Therefore, study your heart to abstract away from the love of visible things and transfer yourself towards invisible things.

29. Homines id quod volunt credunt. (Caesar)
Humans believe the thing which they want.

30. Quod tibi fieri non vis, alteri ne feceris. (Lampridius)
That which you do not want to happen to you, you should not have done to another.

31. Nam qui peccare se nescit, corrigi non vult. (Seneca)
For he who does not know himself to sin, does not want to be corrected.

32. Quid est sapientia? semper idem velle atque idem nolle. (Seneca)
    What is wisdom? Always to want the same thing and not to want the same thing.

33. Pacemne huc fertis an arma? (Virgil)
    Do y'all carry peace or weapons to this place?

34. Volente Deo (Virgil)
    With God willing

35. Afferent montes pacem (episcopal motto)
    The mountains will carry forth peace

36. Domine quid me vis facere (episcopal motto)
    O Lord, what do you want me to do?

37. Surrexit nolite timere (episcopal motto)
    He has risen, do not fear.

38. Deus vult. (motto of the 1st Crusade)
    God wants [it].

39. Omnia fert tempus. (Latin Proverb)
    Time carries all things.

40. Deus meus, volui et legem tuam in medio cordis mei. (*Little Office of the Sacred Heart of Jesus*)
    O my God, I have wanted also your law in the middle of my heart.

41. Aufer tenebras mentium. (Ambrose, *Consors Paterni Luminis*)
    Carry away the shadows of the minds.

42. Splendor paternae gloriae, de luce lucem proferens, lux lucis et fons luminis, diem dies illuminans! (Ambrose, *Splendor Paternae Gloriae*)
    O splendor of paternal glory, bringing forth light down from light, light of light and fountain of light, day illuminating day!

43. Te, satum David, statuit Creator Virginis sponsum, voluitque Verbi te patrem dici, dedit et ministrum esse salutis. (*Caelitum Joseph Decus*)
    The Creator set you, the begotten of David, up to be the husband of the Virgin, and he wanted you to be said to be father of the Word, and he also gave [you] to be a minister of salvation.

44. Liber scriptus proferetur, in quo totum continetur, unde mundus judicetur. (*Dies Irae*)
    The book having been written will be brought forth, in which all is contained, whence the world should be judged.

45. Nos membra confer effici tui beati corporis. (*O Nata Lux de Lumine*)
    Confer us to be made members of your blessed body.

46. Vide Domine afflictionem populi tui, et mitte quem missurus es: emitte Agnum dominatorem terrae, de Petra deserti ad montem filiae Sion: ut auferat ipse jugum captivitatis nostrae. (*Rorate Caeli*)
    O Lord, see the affliction of your people and send him whom you are about to send: send out the Lamb, the dominator of the earth, down from the Rock of the desert towards the mountain of the daughter of Zion, so that the same person might carry away the yoke of our captivity.

47. Consolamini, consolamini, popule meus: cito veniet salus tua... Salvabo te, noli timere, ego enim sum Dominus Deus tuus, Sanctus Israel, Redemptor tuus. (*Rorate Caeli*)
    Be consoled, be consoled, O my people: quickly your salvation will come… I will save you, do not fear, for I am the Lord your God, Holy One of Israel, your Redeemer.

48. Sola digna tu fuisti ferre pretium saeculi. (Venantius Fortunatus, *Pange Lingua*)
    You have been the only worthy one to carry the price of the age. (the 'worthy one' refers to the Cross)

49. Salve ara salve victima, de passionis gloria, qua vita mortem pertulit, et morte vitam reddidit. (Venantius Fortunatus, *Vexilla Regis*)
    Hello, altar, hello Victim, about the glory of the Passion, with which life ended death and [from] death gave back life.

50. Aspiciebam ergo in visione noctis, et ecce cum nubibus caeli quasi filius hominis veniebat, et usque ad antiquum dierum pervenit: et in conspectu ejus obtulerunt eum. Et dedit ei potestatem, et honorem, et regnum: et omnes populi, tribus, et linguae ipsi servient: potestas ejus, potestas aeterna, quae non auferetur: et regnum ejus, quod non corrumpetur. (Dan.7:13-14)
    I was watching therefore in a vision of the night, and behold with the clouds of heaven one as if a son of a human was coming, and he came through all the way towards the ancient one of days, and they offered him in his sight. And he gave to him power, and honor, and the kingdom, and all peoples, tribes, and languages will serve the same; his power is an eternal power, which will not be carried away, and his kingdom is that which will not be corrupted.

51. Et ecce vox de nube, dicens: Hic est Filius meus dilectus, in quo mihi bene complacui: ipsum audite. Et audientes discipuli, ceciderunt in faciem suam et timuerunt valde. Et accessit Jesus et tetigit eos, dixitque eos Surgite, et nolite timere. Levantes autem oculos suos, neminem viderunt nisi solum Jesum. Et descendentibus illis de monte, praecepit eis Jesus, dicens: Nemini dixeritis visionem, donec Filius hominis a mortuis resurgat. (Mt.17:5-9)
And behold, a voice down from the cloud, saying, "This is my beloved Son, in whom I have been well pleased to myself; hear the same." And the disciples, hearing, fell on their face and feared very much. And Jesus approached and touched them and said to them, "Rise, and do not fear." However, lifting their eyes, they saw no one except Jesus alone. And, with them descending down from the mountain, Jesus commanded them, saying, "You should have said to no one the vision, until the Son of a human should rise from the dead."

52. Memorare, O piissima Virgo Maria, non esse auditum a saeculo, quemquam ad tua currentem praesidia, tua implorantem auxilia, tua petentem suffragia, esse derelictum. Ego tali animatus confidentia, ad te, Virgo Virginum, Mater, curro, ad te venio, coram te gemens peccator assisto. Noli, Mater Verbi, verba mea despicere; sed audi propitia et exaudi. Amen. (Catholic Prayer)
Remember, O most pious Virgin Mary, it not to be having been heard from an age, whomever running towards your protection, imploring your help, seeking your approval, to be abandoned. Having been inspired with thus confidence, towards you, Virgin of virgins, Mother, I run, towards you I come, before you I take a stand, a groaning sinner. O Mother of the Word, do not despise my words, but, being favorable, hear and listen. Amen.

Chapter Twenty-seven

1. Et intellexi quod omnium operum Dei nullam possit homo invenire rationem eorum quae fiunt sub sole, et quanto plus laboraverit ad quaerendum, tanto minus inveniat. (Ecc.8:17)
And I understood that of all the deeds of God a human should be able to find no reason of them which happen under the sun, and how much more he should have worked to seek, so much less he should find.

2. Illum oportet crescere, me autem minui. (Jn.3:30)
It is necessary him to grow, me however to diminish.

3. Beatius est magis dare quam accipere. (Acts.20:35)
It is more blessed more to give than to receive.

4. Et dixit mihi: Haec verba fidelissima sunt, et vera. Et Dominus Deus spirituum prophetarum misit angelum suum ostendere servis suis quae oportet fieri cito. Et ecce venio velociter. Beatus, qui custodit verba prophetiae libri hujus. (Rev.22:6-7)
    And he said to me: These words are most faithful and true. And the Lord God of the spirits of the prophets has sent his angel to show to his servants those things which it is necessary to happen quickly. And behold, I am coming quickly. Blessed is he who guards the words of the prophecy of this book.

5. Diligo te, o Bonitas infinita, amo te plus quam me; et quia amo te, dono tibi corpus meum, animam meam, ac totam voluntatem meam. (Alphonsus Liguori)
    I love you, O infinite goodness, I love you more than myself, and because I love you, I grant to you my body, my soul, and all my will.

6. Fac ut magis ac magis tuam bonitatem et amorem, qui tibi debetur, et caritatem, qua me dilexisti, semper agnoscam. (Alphonsus Liguori)
    Make that I might always realize more and more your goodness and the love which is owed to you and the charity, with which you have loved me.

7. Credo Domine, sed credam firmius; spero, sed sperem securius; amo, sed amem ardentius; doleo, sed doleam vehementius. (Clement XI)
    I believe, O Lord, but would that I might believe more firmly; I hope, but would that I might hope more securely; I love, but would that I might love more ardently; I mourn, but would that I might mourn more vehemently.

8. Aperite plene portas Christo. (John Paul the Great)
    Open fully the gates to Christ.

9. Certe adveniente die judicii, non quaeretur a nobis quid legimus, sed quid fecimus; nec quam bene diximus, sed quam religiose viximus. (a Kempis)
    Certainly, on the coming day of judgment, it will not be sought from us what we read but what we did, nor how well we said, but how religiously we lived.

10. Dignare, Domine manere mecum, ego volo libenter esse tecum. Hoc est totum desiderium meum, ut cor meum tibi sit unitum. (a Kempis)
    Deign, O Lord, to remain with me: I freely want to be with you. This is all my desire, that my heart should be united to you.

11. Omnis homo naturaliter scire desiderat. (a Kempis)
    Every human naturally desires to know.

12. Qui vero saepius orare voluerit, uberiorem inveniet misericordiam Christi. (Macarius of Alexandria)
    He who should have wanted truly to pray more often, will find richer mercy of Christ.

13. Similiter quoque omnes oportet diligere fratres, cum quibus etiam te confidis videre gloriam Christi. (Macarius of Alexandria)
    Similarly, all also ought to love the brothers with whom also you trust yourself to see the glory of Christ.

14. Conjugalis amor et fidelis et exclusorius est, usque ad vitae extremum. (Paul VI)
    Conjugal and faithful love is also most exclusive, all the way towards the end of life.

15. Minuit praesentia famam. (Claudian)
    Presence diminishes fame.

16. Vis recte vivere? Quis non? (Horace)
    You want to live rightly? Who doesn't?

17. Qui timide rogat, docet negare. (Seneca)
    He who asks timidly, teaches to deny.

18. Caritate fortiter et suaviter (episcopal motto)
    With love more strongly and more sweetly

19. Credam firmius (episcopal motto)
    I will believe more firmly.

20. Fideliter praedicare evangelium Christi (episcopal motto)
    To faithfully preach the Gospel of Christ

21. Humiliter in lumine vultus tui (episcopal motto)
    Humbly in the light of your face

22. Bis dat, qui cito dat. (Latin proverb)
    He gives twice who gives quickly.

23. Qui immoderate omnia cupiunt, saepe in totum frustrantur. (Latin Proverb)
    They who desire all things immoderately, are often frustrated in all.

24. Amo te, o Jesu, mi Amor, magis quam meipsum, et ex intimo corde paenitet me quod tibi displicui. Ne sinas me iterum a te separari. Da mihi perpetuum amorem tui, et dein fac de me quidquid tibi placuerit. (Alphonsus Liguori, *Way of the Cross*)
    I love you, O Jesus, my Love, more than myself, and out of the inner heart I repent that which I displeased you. Do not permit me again to be separated from you. Give to me a perpetual love of you and then do about me whatever will have been pleasing to you.

25. Me de manu hostium potenter defende. (*Little Office of the Immaculate Conception*)
    Defend me powerfully down from the hand of the enemies.

26. Adoro te devote, latens Deitas, quae sub his figuris vere latitas; tibi se cor meum totum subjicit, quia te contemplans totum deficit. (Aquinas, *Adoro Te Devote*)
I adore you devotely, Deity being hidden, you who under these figures truly lurk. All my heart subjects itself to you, because, contemplating you, all fails.

27. O memoriale mortis Domini! Panis vivus, vitam praestans homini! Praesta meae menti de te vivere, et te illi semper dulce sapere. (Aquinas, *Adoro Te Devote*)
O memorial of the death of the Lord! Alive bread, bestowing life to human! Bestow to my mind to live about you, and to that to sweetly taste you always. (illi refers to menti)

28. Nil canitur suavius, nil auditur jucundius, nil cogitatur dulcius quam Jesus Dei Filius. (Bernard, *Jesu Dulcis Memoria*)
Nothing more sweetly to be sung about, nothing more pleasant to be heard, nothing more sweetly to be thought than Jesus the Son of God.

29. Nocte surgentes vigilemus omnes, semper in psalmis meditemur atque viribus totis Domino canamus dulciter hymnos. (Gregory the Great, *Nocte Surgentes Vigilemus*)
Rising at night, let us all keep vigil; let us meditate always on the psalms and let us sweetly sing about hymns to the Lord with all the (our) strengths.

30. O certe necessarium Adae peccatum, quod Christi morte deletum est. O felix culpa, quae talem ac tantum meruit habere Redemptorem. O vere beata nox, quae sola meruit scire tempus et horam in qua Christus ab inferis resurrexit. Haec nox est, de qua scriptum est: Et nox sicut dies illuminabitur. (Exsultet)
O certainly necessary sin of Adam, which has been deleted with the death of Christ. O happy fault, which merited to have such and so great a Redeemer. O truly blessed night, which alone merited to know the time and hour on which Christ rose from the underworld. This is the night, about which it is having been written: And the night will be illumined like the day.

31. Ubi caritas et amor, Deus ibi est. Congregavit nos in unum Christi amor. Exsultemus, et in ipso jucundemur. Timeamus, et amemus Deum vivum. Et ex corde diligamus nos sincero. Simul ergo cum in unum congregamur: Ne nos mente dividamur... Et in medio nostri sit Christus Deus. Simul quoque cum beatis videamus, glorianter vultum tuum, Christe Deus: Gaudium quod est immensum, atque probum, saecula per infinita saeculorum. Amen. (Holy Thursday Antiphon)
Where there is charity and love, God is there. Love of Christ has congregated us into one. Let us exalt and be glad in the same. Let us fear and love the alive God, and may we love out of the heart, sincerely. At the same time, therefore, when into one we are gathered: let us not be divided with (regards to) the mind. And may Christ, God, be in the midst of us. At the same time also may we see your face gloriously with the blessed ones, O Christ God: a joy which is immense and righteous through infinite ages of ages. Amen.

Chapter Twenty-eight

1. Si dormiero, dicam: Quando consurgam? (Job.7:4)
   If I will have slept, I will say, "When shall I arise?"

2. Peccavi; quid faciam tibi, o custos hominum? Cur non tollis peccatum meum? (Job.7:20, 21)
   I have sinned; what will I do to you, O guard of humans? Why do you not take away my sin?

3. Beati qui esuriunt et sitiunt justitiam: quoniam ipsi saturabuntur. (Mt.5:6)
   Blessed are they who hunger and thirst (for) justice: because the same will be saturated.

4. Ego autem dico vobis: diligite inimicos vestros, benefacite his qui oderunt vos. (Mt.5:44)
   However, I say to y'all: love your enemies, bless these who hate y'all.

5. Esurientes implevit bonis. (Lk.1:53)
   He has filled the hungering ones with good things.

6. Ignem veni mittere in terram et quid volo si accendatur. (Lk.12:49)
   I came to send fire into the earth and what do I want if it should be kindled!

7. Ego sum panis vivus, qui de caelo descendi. Si quis manducaverit ex hoc pane, vivet in aeternum: et panis quem ego dabo, caro mea est pro mundi vita. (Jn.6:51-52)
   I am the alive bread which has descended down from heaven. If [any]one will have eaten out of this bread, he will live into eternity; and the bread which I will give is my flesh for the life of the world.

8. Qui amat animam suam, perdet eam; et qui odit animam suam in hoc mundo, in vitam aeternam custodit eam. (Jn.12:25)
   He who loves his own soul, will lose it; and whoever hates his own soul in this world, into eternal life guards it.

9. Respondit Jesus, et dixit ei: Si quis diligit me, sermonem meum servabit, et Pater meus diliget eum, et ad eum veniemus. (Jn.14:23)
   Jesus responded and said to him, "If [any]one loves me, he will keep my word, and my Father will love him, and we will come towards him."

10. Si Deus pro nobis, quis contra nos? (Rom.8:31)
    If God is for us, who is against us?

11. Deum nemo vidit umquam. Si diligamus invicem, Deus in nobis manet, et caritas ejus in nobis perfecta est. In hoc cognoscimus quoniam in eo manemus, et ipse in nobis: quoniam de Spiritu suo dedit nobis. (1Jn.4:12-13)
    No one has ever seen God. If we should love one another, God remains in us, and his charity has been perfected in us. In this we recognize that we remain in him, and the same in us: because about his own Spirit he has given to us.

12. Cum dilectione hominum et odio vitiorum. (Augustine)
    With love of humans and hatred of vices.

13. Quid est ergo tempus? Si nemo ex me quaerat, scio; si quaerenti explicare velim, nescio. (Augustine)
    What is time, therefore? If no one should seek (it) out of me, I know; if I should want to explain to the one seeking, I do not know.

14. Si sapientia Deus est, verus philosophus est amator Dei. (Augustine)
    If wisdom is God, a true philosopher is a lover of God.

15. Si vis amari, ama. (Augustine)
    If you want to be loved, love.

16. Conari debemus per speculum videre Deum. (Bonaventure)
    We ought to try to see God through a mirror.

17. Scriptura sacra mentis oculis quasi quoddam speculum opponitur, ut interna nostra facies in ipsa videatur. Ibi etenim foeda, ibi pulchra nostra cognoscimus. (Gregory the Great)
    Sacred Scripture is placed towards the eyes of the mind as if a certain mirror, so that our internal face might be seen in the same. As a matter of fact, we recognize there our vile things, there our beautiful things.

18. Haec est altissima et utilissima lectio. (a Kempis about the Bible)
    This is the highest and most useful reading.

19. Cum odio sui coepit veritas. (Tertullian)
    Truth begins with hatred of oneself.

20. Si vis me flere, dolendum est primum ipsi tibi. (Horace)
    If you want me to weep, these same must first be mourned by you.

21. Parcere personis, dicere de vitiis. (Martial)
    To spare the persons, to speak about the vices

22. Fit culpa si iterum cecideris. (Publilius Syrus)
    A fault would happen if you should have fallen again.

23. Veritas odit moras. (Seneca)
    Truth hates delays.

24. Si vales bene est, ego valeo. (beginning of Roman letters)
    If you are strong, it is well; I am strong.

25. Verbum caro, panem verum, verbo carnem efficit: fitque sanguis Christi merum, et si sensus deficit, ad firmandum cor sincerum, sola fides sufficit. (Aquinas, *Pange Lingua*)
    The Word is flesh, it makes bread by the word true flesh, and the blood of Christ becomes undiluted wine, and if the sense fails, in order to firm up a sincere heart, only faith suffices.

26. Somno si dantur oculi, cor semper ad te vigilet; tuaque dextra protegas, fideles qui te diligunt. (*Christe qui Splendor et Dies*)
    If the eyes are given to sleep, may the heart always keep vigil towards you, and with your right hand may you protect the faithful who love you.

27. Quis est homo qui non fleret, Christi matrem si videret, in tanto supplicio? Quis non posset contristari, piam matrem contemplari, dolentem cum filio? (*Stabat Mater Dolorosa*)
    Who is the human who would not be weeping, if he were seeing the mother of Christ in so great suffering? Who would not be able to be saddened, to contemplate the pious mother mourning with the Son.

28. Quisquam est, qui non gauderet, Christi matrem si videret in tanto solatio? (*Stabat Mater Speciosa*)
    Is there anyone who would not rejoice, if he were seeing the mother of Christ in so great solace?

29. Si autem quaeras, quomodo haec fiant, interroga gratiam, non doctrinam; desiderium, non intellectum; gemitum orationis, non studium lectionis; sponsum, non magistrum; Deum non hominem: caliginem non claritatem; non lucem, sed ignem. (Bonaventure describing the journey to God)
    However, if you should seek how these things should happen, interrogate grace, not doctrine, desire, not understanding, the groaning of prayer, not the study of readings, a spouse, not a teacher, God, not a human, gloom not clarity, not light, but fire.

30. O pura et immaculata, eadem benedicta Virgo, magni Filii tui universorum Domini Mater inculpata, integra et sacrosanctissima, desperantium atque reorum spes, te collaudamus. Tibi ut gratia plenissimae benedicimus, quae Christum genuisti Deum et Hominem: omnes coram te prosternimur: omnes te invocamus et auxilium tuum imploramus. (Catholic Prayer)
O pure and immaculate, the same blessed Virgin, Mother of your great Son, Lord of all things: not having been faulted, whole, and most holily-sacred, hope of the despairing and of the guilty, we praise you together. We bless you as most full with grace, who gave birth to Christ, God and human. We all are prostrated before you, we all invoke you and implore your help.

Chapter Twenty-nine

1. Feceruntque filii Levi juxta sermonem Moysi, cecideruntque in die illa quasi viginti tria millia hominum. (Ex.32:28)
And the sons of Levi did according to the word of Moses, and on that day fell as if twenty-three thousand humans.

2. Dormivit igitur David cum patribus suis, et sepultus est in civitate David. Dies autem quibus regnavit David super Israel, quadraginta anni sunt: in Hebron regnavit septem annis; in Jerusalem, triginta tribus. (1Kgs.2:10-11)
Therefore David slept with his own fathers and was buried in the city of David. However, the days with which David reigned over Israel are forty years: in Hebron he reigned seven years, in Jerusalem, thirty-three.

3. Dies autem quos regnavit Salomon in Jerusalem super omnem Israel, quadraginta anni sunt. (1Kgs.11:42)
However, the days which Solomon reigned in Jerusalem over all Israel are forty years.

4. In anno ergo vigesimo Jeroboam regis Israel regnavit Asa rex Juda, et quadraginta et uno anno regnavit in Jerusalem. Nomen matris ejus Maacha filia Abessalom. (1Kgs.15:9-10)
Therefore, in the twentieth year of Jeroboam king of Israel, Asa king of Judah reigned, and he reigned forty and one year in Jerusalem. The name of his mother is Maacah daughter of Absalom.

5. Anno tertio Asa regis Juda, regnavit Baasa filius Ahiae super omnem Israel in Thersa, viginti quatuor annis. (1Kgs.15:33)
In the third year of Asa king of Judah, Baasha son of Ahijah reigned over all Israel in Tirzah, twenty-four years.

6. Anno vigesimo sexto Asa regis Juda, regnavit Ela filius Baasa super Israel in Thersa, duobus annis. (1Kgs.16:8)
   In the twenty-sixth year of Asa king of Judah, Elah son of Baasha reigned over Israel in Tirzah, two years.

7. Anno vigesimo septimo Asa regis Juda, regnavit Zambri septem diebus in Thersa. (1Kgs.16:15)
   In the twenty-seventh year of Asa, king of Judah, Zimri reigned seven days in Tirzah.

8. Achab vero filius Amri regnavit super Israel anno trigesimo octavo Asa regis Juda; et regnavit Achab filius Amri super Israel in Samaria viginti et duobus annis. (1Kgs.16:29)
   Truly Ahab son of Omri reigned over Israel in the thirty-eighth year of Asa king of Judah, and Ahab son of Omri reigned over Israel in Samaria twenty and two years.

9. Joram vero filius Achab regnavit super Israel in Samaria anno decimooctavo Josaphat regis Judae: regnavitque duodecim annis. (2Kgs.3:1)
   Truly, Joram son of Ahab reigned over Israel in Samaria in the eighteenth year of Jehoshaphat king of Judah, and he reigned twelve years.

10. Anno quinto Joram filii Achab regis Israel, et Josaphat regis Juda, regnavit Joram filius Josaphat rex Juda. Triginta duorum annorum erat cum regnare coepisset, et octo annis regnavit in Jerusalem. (2Kgs.8:16-17)
    In the fifth year of Joram son of Ahab king of Israel and Jehoshaphat king of Judah, reigned Joram son of Jehoshaphat king of Judah. Of thirty-two years (old) he was when he would begin to reign, and eight years he reigned in Jerusalem.

11. Anno duodecimo Joram filii Achab regis Israel regnavit Ochozias filius Joram regis Judae. Viginti duorum annorum erat Ochozias cum regnare coepisset, et uno anno regnavit in Jerusalem. (2Kgs.8:25-26)
    In the twelfth year of Joram son of Ahab king of Israel, Ahaziah son of Joram king of Judah reigned. Ahaziah was of twenty-two years when he would begin to reign, and he reigned one year in Jerusalem.

12. Erant autem Achab septuaginta filii in Samaria. (2Kgs.10:1)
    However, to Ahab were seventy sons in Samaria.

13. Anno septimo Jehu, regnavit Joas: et quadraginta annis regnavit in Jerusalem. Nomen matris ejus Sebia de Bersabee. (2Kgs.12:1)
    In the seventh year of Jehu, Joash reigned, and he reigned forty years in Jerusalem. The name of his mother was Zibiah about (of) Beersheba.

14. Anno vigesimo tertio Joas filii Ochoziae regis Juda, regnavit Joachaz filius Jehu super Israel in Samaria decem et septem annis. (2Kgs.13:1)
    In the twenty-third year of Joash son of Ahaziah king of Judah, Jehoahaz son of Jehu reigned over Israel in Samaria ten and seven (seventeen) years.

15. Anno trigesimo septimo Joas regis Juda, regnavit Joas filius Joachaz super Israel in Samaria sedecim annis. (2Kgs.13:10)
    In the thirty-seventh year of Joash king of Judah, Joash son of Jehoahaz reigned over Israel in Samaria sixteen years.

16. In anno secundo Joas filii Joachaz regis Israel, regnavit Amasias filius Joas regis Juda. Viginti quinque annorum erat cum regnare coepisset: viginti autem et novem annis regnavit in Jerusalem. Nomen matris ejus Joadan de Jerusalem. (2Kgs.14:1-2)
    In the second year of Joash son of Jehoahaz king of Israel, Amaziah son of Joash king of Judah reigned. He was of twenty-five years when he would begin to reign, however twenty-nine years he reigned in Jerusalem. The name of his mother was Jehoaddin about Jerusalem.

17. Anno quintodecimo Amasiae filii Joas regis Juda, regnavit Jeroboam filius Joas regis Israel in Samaria, quadraginta et uno anno. (2Kgs.14:23)
    In the fifteenth year of Amaziah son of Joash king of Judah, Jeroboam son of Joash king of Israel reigned in Samaria forty and one year.

18. Anno vigesimo septimo Jeroboam regis Israel, regnavit Azarias filius Amasiae regis Juda. Sedecim annorum erat cum regnare coepisset, et quinquaginta duobus annis regnavit in Jerusalem: nomen matris ejus Jechelia de Jerusalem. (2Kgs.15:1-2)
    In the twenty-seventh year of Jeroboam king of Israel, Azariah son of Amaziah king of Judah reigned. He was of sixteen years when he would begin to reign, and he reigned fifty-two years in Jerusalem; the name of his mother was Jecoliah about Jerusalem.

19. Anno trigesimo octavo Azariae regis Juda, regnavit Zacharias filius Jeroboam super Israel in Samaria sex mensibus. (2Kgs.15:8)
    In the thirty-eighth year of Azariah king of Judah, Zechariah son of Jeroboam reigned over Israel in Samaria six months.

20. Sellum filius Jabes regnavit trigesimo novo anno Azariae regis Juda: regnavit autem uno mense in Samaria. (2Kgs.15:13)
    Shallum son of Jabesh reigned in the thirty-ninth year of Azariah king of Judah, however he reigned one month in Samaria.

21. Anno trigesimo nono Azariae regis Juda, regnavit Manahem filius Gadi super Israel decem annis in Samaria. (2Kgs.15:17)
    In the thirty-ninth year of Azariah king of Judah, Menahem son of Gadi reigned over Israel ten years in Samaria.

22. Anno quinquagesimo Azariae regis Juda, regnavit Phaceia filius Manahem super Israel in Samaria biennio. (2Kgs.15:23)
In the fiftieth year of Azariah king of Judah, Pekahiah son of Menahem reigned over Israel in Samaria two years.

23. Anno quinquagesimo secundo Azariae regis Juda, regnavit Phacee filius Romeliae super Israel in Samaria viginti annis. (2Kgs.15:27)
In the fifty-second year of Azariah king of Judah, Pekah son of Remaliah reigned over Israel in Samaria twenty years.

24. Anno secundo Phacee filii Romeliae regis Israel, regnavit Joatham filius Oziae regis Juda. Viginti quinque annorum erat cum regnare coepisset, et sedecim annis regnavit in Jerusalem: nomen matris ejus Jerusa filia Sadoc. (2Kgs.15:32-33)
In the second year of Pekah son of Remaliah king of Israel, Jotham son of Uzziah king of Judah reigned. He was of twenty-five years when he would begin to reign, and he reigned sixteen years in Jerusalem. The name of his mother was Jerusha daughter of Zadok.

25. Anno decimoseptimo Phacee filii Romeliae, regnavit Achaz filius Joatham regis Juda. Viginti annorum erat Achaz cum regnare coepisset, et sedecim annis regnavit in Jerusalem. (2Kgs.16:1-2)
In the seventeenth year of Pekah son of Remaliah, Ahaz son of Jotham king of Judah reigned. Ahaz was of twenty years when he would begin to reign, and he reigned sixteen years in Jerusalem.

26. Anno duodecimo Achaz regis Juda, regnavit Osee filius Ela in Samaria super Israel novem annis. (2Kgs.17:1)
In the twelfth year of Ahaz king of Judah, Hoshea son of Elah reigned in Samaria over Israel nine years.

27. Anno tertio Osee filii Ela regis Israel, regnavit Ezechias filius Achaz regis Juda. Viginti quinque annorum erat cum regnare coepisset, et viginti novem annis regnavit in Jerusalem: nomen matris ejus Abi filia Zachariae. (2Kgs.18:1-2)
In the third year of Hoshea son of Elah king of Israel, Hezekiah son of Ahaz king of Judah reigned. He was of twenty-five years when he would begin to reign, and he reigned twenty-nine years in Jerusalem. The name of his mother was Abi daughter of Zechariah.

28. Duodecim annorum erat Manasses cum regnare coepisset, et quinquaginta quinque annis regnavit in Jerusalem: nomen matris ejus Haphsiba. (2Kgs.21:1)
Manasseh was of twelve years when he would begin to reign, and he reigned fifty-five years in Jerusalem. The name of his mother was Hephzibah.

29. Octo annorum erat Josias cum regnare coepisset: triginta et uno anno regnavit in Jerusalem: nomen matris ejus Idida filia Hadaja de Besecath. (2Kgs.22:1)
Josiah was of eight years when he would begin to reign; he reigned thirty and one year in Jerusalem. The name of his mother was Jedidah daughter of Adaiah about (of) Bozkath.

30. Viginti trium annorum erat Joachaz cum regnare coepisset, et tribus mensibus regnavit in Jerusalem: nomen matris ejus Amital filia Jeremiae de Lobna. (2Kgs.23:31)
Jehoahaz was of twenty-three years when he would begin to reign, and he reigned three months in Jerusalem. The name of his mother was Hamutal daughter of Jeremiah about Libnah.

31. Viginti quinque annorum erat Joakim cum regnare coepisset, et undecim annis regnavit in Jerusalem: nomen matris ejus Zebida filia Phadaja de Ruma. (2Kgs.23:36)
Jehoiakim was of twenty-five years when he would begin to reign, and he reigned eleven years in Jerusalem. The name of his mother was Zebidah daughter of Pedaiah about Rumah.

32. Decem et octo annorum erat Joachin cum regnare coepisset, et tribus mensibus regnavit in Jerusalem: nomen matris ejus Nohesta filia Elnathan de Jerusalem. (2Kgs.24:8)
Jehoiachin was of ten and eight years when he would begin to reign, and he reigned three months in Jerusalem. The name of his mother was Nehushta daughter of Elnathan about Jerusalem.

33. Vox dilecti mei! Ecce iste venit! (SS.2:8)
The voice of my beloved! Behold, he comes!

34. Dilectus meus mihi, et ego illi. (SS.2:16)
My beloved is to me (is mine), and I to him.

35. Quam pulchra es, amica mea; quam pulchra es! (SS.4:1)
How beautiful you are, my girl-friend, how beautiful you are!

36. Qualis est dilectus tuus ex dilecto, o pulcherrima mulierum? Qualis est dilectus tuus ex dilecto, quia sic adjurasti nos? Dilectus meus candidus et rubicundus, electus ex millibus. (SS.5:9-10)
What sort is your beloved out of [any other] beloved, O most beautiful of women? What sort is your beloved out of [any other] beloved, that you have adjured us thus? My beloved is radiant and rugged, chosen out of thousands.

37. Sexaginta sunt reginae, et octoginta concubinae, et adolescentularum non est numerus. Una est columba mea, perfecta mea, una est matris suae, electa genetrici suae. Viderunt eam filiae, et beatissimam praedicaverunt, reginae et concubinae, et laudaverunt eam. (SS.6:7-8)
There are sixty queens and eighty concubines and of adolescent girls there is not a number. One is my dove, my perfect one; she is [the only] one of her mother, the chosen one to her one-who-gave-birth-to-her. The daughters have seen her and have proclaimed her most blessed; the queens and concubines have also praised her.

38. Quam pulchra es, et quam decora, carissima! (SS.7:6)
How beautiful you are, and how honored, O dearest one!

39. Pone me ut signaculum super cor tuum, ut signaculum super brachium tuum, quia fortis est ut mors dilectio. (SS.8:6)
Put me as a little sign over your heart, as a little sign over your arm, because strong as death is love.

40. Aspiciebam donec throni positi sunt, et antiquus dierum sedit… Millia millium ministrabant ei. (Dan.7:9-10)
I was watching until thrones are having been placed and the ancient of days sat. Thousands of thousands were ministering to him.

41. Omnes itaque generationes ab Abraham usque ad David, generationes quatuordecim: et a David usque ad transmigrationem Babylonis, generationes quatuordecim: et a transmigratione Babylonis usque ad Christum, generationes quatuordecim. (Mt.1:17)
And thus all the generations from Abraham all the way towards David were fourteen generations, and from David all the way towards the migration across to Babylon, fourteen generations, and from the migration across to Babylon all the way towards Christ, fourteen generations.

42. Propter hoc relinquet homo patrem suum et matrem, et adhaerebit ad uxorem suam: et erunt duo in carne una. Itaque jam non sunt duo, sed una caro. Quod ergo Deus conjunxit, homo non separet. (Mk.10:7-9)
Because of this a human relinquishes his own father and mother and adheres towards his own wife, and two will be in one flesh. And thus they are not now two, but one flesh. Therefore, what God has joined together, a human may not separate.

43. Multi autem erunt primi novissimi, et novissimi primi. (Mk.10:31)
Many first, however, will be the newest, and the newest first.

44. Quicumque voluerit fieri major, erit vester minister: et quicumque voluerit in vobis primus esse, erit omnium servus. (Mk.10:43-44)
Whosoever should have wanted to become greater, he shall be your minister, and whosoever should have wanted to be first in y'all shall be the servant of all.

45. Et vidi: et ecce Agnus stabat supra montem Sion, et cum eo centum quadraginta quatuor millia. (Rev.14:1)
    And I saw, and behold the Lamb was standing over the mountain of Zion, and with him a hundred forty-four thousands.

46. Et vixerunt, et regnaverunt cum Christo mille annis. (Rev.20:4)
    And they lived and reigned with Christ a thousand years.

47. Ego sum alpha et omega, primus et novissimus, principium et finis. (Rev.22:13)
    I am the alpha and the omega, the first and the newest, the beginning and the end.

48. Nolite timere: quinta enim die veniet ad vos Dominus noster. (Advent Antiphon)
    Do not fear, for on the fifth day our Lord will come towards y'all.

49. In principio primum principium, a quo cunctae illuminationes descendunt tanquam a Patre luminum, a quo est omne datum optimum et omne donum perfectum. (beginning of Bonaventure's *Journey of the Mind into God*)
    In the beginning was the first beginning, from which all lights descend just as from the Father of lights, from which is every best thing given and every perfect gift.

50. O eterne Deus, nunc tibi placeat, ut in amore illo ardeas, ut membra illa simus quae fecisti in eodem amore, cum Filium tuum genuisti in prima aurora ante omnem creaturam: et inspice necessitatem hanc. (Hildegard)
    O eternal God, now may it be pleasing to you so that you might burn in that love so that we may be those members which you made in the same love, when you begot your Son in the first dawn before every creature, and inspect this necessity.

51. Non possunt primi esse omnes omni in tempore. (Laberius)
    They are not all able to be first in every time.

52. Cur non mitto meos tibi Pontiliane libellos? Ne mihi tu mittas Pontiliane tuos. (Martial)
    Why do I not send my little books to you, Pontilian? So that you might not send yours to me, Pontilian.

53. Primus in orbe deos fecit timor. (Petronius)
    Fear first made gods in the world.

54. Christus primus (episcopal motto)
    First Christ

55. Fides, spes, caritas, tria haec (episcopal motto)
    Faith, hope, charity, these three.

56. Quaerite prime regnum Dei. (motto of Newfoundland)
    Seek first the kingdom of God.

57. Sumit unus, sumunt mille: quantum isti, tantum ille, nec sumptus consumitur. (Aquinas, *Lauda Sion*)
    One receives, a thousand receives, as much these, so much that, neither is consumed the one received.

58. In supremae nocte coenae, recumbens cum fratribus, observata lege plene, cibis in legalibus, cibum turbae duodenae se dat suis manibus. (Aquinas, *Pange Lingua*)
    In the night of the supreme (final) dinner, reclining with brothers, with the full law having been observed, in the lawful foods, he gave himself with his own hands (as) food to the crowd of twelve.

59. Sit laus Deo Patri, summo Christo decus, Spiritui Sancto, tribus honor unus. (*Ave Maris Stella*)
    Let praise be to God the Father, glory to the highest Christ, to the Holy Spirit, to the three one honor.

60. Duo Seraphim clamabant alter ad alterum: Sanctus, Sanctus, Sanctus Dominus Deus Sabaoth. Plena est omnis terra gloria ejus. Tres sunt qui testimonium dant in caelo: Pater, et Verbum, et Spiritus Sanctus: hi tres unum sunt. Sanctus, Sanctus, Sanctus Dominus Deus Sabaoth. Plena est omnis terra gloria ejus. (*Duo Seraphim*)
    Two Seraphim were shouting one towards another: Holy, holy, holy is the Lord God of Hosts. Full is every land with his glory. There are three who give testimony in heaven: Father and Word and Holy Spirit--these three are one. Holy, holy, holy is the Lord God of Hosts. Full is every land with his glory.

61. Qui est imago Dei invisibilis, primogenitus omnis creaturae: quoniam in ipso condita sunt universa in caelis, et in terra, visibilia, et invisibilia... omnia per ipsum et in ipso creata sunt: et ipse est ante omnes, et omnia in ipso constant. Et ipse est caput corporis Ecclesiae, qui est principium, primogenitus ex mortuis: ut sit in omnibus ipse primatum tenens. (Col.1:15-18)
    He who is the image of the invisible God, the firstborn of every creature, because in the same all things are having been built in the heavens and on earth, the visible and the invisible. All things are having been created through the same and in the same, and the same is before all, and all things stand together in the same. And the same is the head of the body, the Church, who is the beginning, the firstborn out of the dead ones, so that in all things the same might be holding primacy.

62. Qui venerunt cum Zorobabel, Josue, Nehemia, Saraia, Rahelaia, Mardochai, Belsan, Mesphar, Beguai, Rehum, Baana. Numerus virorum populi Israel: filii Pharos duo millia centum septuaginta duo. Filii Sephatia, trecenti septuaginta duo. Filii Area, septingenti septuaginta quinque. Filii Phahath Moab, filiorum Josue: Joab, duo millia octingenti duodecim. Filii Aelam, mille ducenti quinquaginta quatuor. Filii Zethua, nongenti quadraginta quinque. Filii Zachai, septingenti sexaginta. Filii Bani, sexcenti quadraginta duo. Filii Bebai, sexcenti viginti tres. Filii Azgad, mille ducenti viginti duo. Filii Adonicam, sexcenti sexaginta sex. Filii Beguai, duo millia quinquaginta sex. Filii Adin, quadringenti quinquaginta quatuor. Filii Ather, qui erant ex Ezechia, nonaginta octo. Filii Besai, trecenti viginti tres. Filii Jora, centum duodecim. Filii Hasum, ducenti viginti tres. Filii Gebbar, nonaginta quinque. Filii Bethlehem, centum viginti tres. Viri Netupha, quinquaginta sex. Viri Anathoth, centum viginti octo. Filii Azmaveth, quadraginta duo. Filii Cariathiarim, Cephira et Beroth, septingenti quadraginta tres. Filii Rama et Gabaa, sexcenti viginti unus. Viri Machmas, centum viginti duo. Viri Bethel et Hai, ducenti viginti tres. Filii Nebo, quinquaginta duo. Filii Megbis, centum quinquaginta sex. Filii Aelam alterius, mille ducenti quinquaginta quatuor. Filii Harim, trecenti viginti. Filii Lod Hadid, et Ono, septingenti viginti quinque. Filii Jericho, trecenti quadraginta quinque. Filii Senaa, tria millia sexcenti triginta. Sacerdotes: filii Jadaia in domo Josue, nongenti septuaginta tres. Filii Emmer, mille quinquaginta duo. Filii Pheshur, mille ducenti quadraginta septem. Filii Harim, mille decem et septem. Levitae: filii Josue et Cedmihel filiorum Odoviae, septuaginta quatuor. Cantores: filii Asaph, centum viginti octo.
(Ezr.2:2-41)

Those who came with Zerubbabel: Jeshua, Nehemiah, Seraiah, Reelaiah, Mordecai, Bilshan, Mispar, Bigvai, Rehum, Baanah. The number of the men of the people of Israel: the sons of Parosh, two thousands one hundred seventy-two. The sons of Shephatiah, three hundred and seventy-two. The sons of Arah, seven hundred seventy-five. The sons of Pahath-moab, of the sons of Jeshua, Joab, two thousands eight hundred twelve. The sons of Elam, a thousand two hundred fifty-four. The sons of Zattu, nine hundred forty-five. The sons of Zaccai, seven hundred sixty. The sons of Bani, six hundred forty-two. The sons of Bebai, six hundred twenty-three. The sons of Azgad, a thousand two hundred twenty-two. The sons of Adonikam, six hundred sixty-six. The sons of Bigvai, two thousands fifty-six. The sons of Adin, four hundred fifty-four. The sons of Ater, who was out of Hezekiah, ninety-eight. The sons of Bezai, three hundred twenty-three. The sons of Jorah, one hundred twelve. The sons of Hashum, two hundred twenty-three. The sons of Gibbar, ninety-five. The sons of Bethlehem, one hundred twenty-three. The men of Netophah, fifty-six. The men of Anathoth, one hundred twenty-eight. The sons of Azmaveth, forty-two. The sons of Kiriatharim, Chephirah, and Beeroth, seven hundred forty-three. The sons of Ramah and Geba, six hundred twenty-one. The men of Michmas, one hundred twenty-two. The men of Bethel and Ai, two hundred twenty-three. The sons of Nebo, fifty-two. The sons of Magbish, one hundred fifty-six. The sons of the other Elam, one thousand two hundred fifty-four. The sons of Harim, three hundred twenty. The sons of Lod, Hadid, and Ono, seven hundred twenty-five. The sons of Jericho, three hundred forty-five. The sons of Senaah, three thousand six hundred thirty. The priests: the sons of Jedaiah in the house of

Jeshua, nine hundred seventy-three. The sons of Immer, one thousand fifty-two. The sons of Pashhur, one thousand two hundred forty-seven. The sons of Harim, one thousand seventeen. The Levites: the sons of Jeshua and Kadmiel of the sons of Hodaviah, seventy-four. The singers: the sons of Asaph, one hundred twenty-eight.

Chapter Thirty

1. Dixitque Cain ad Abel fratrem suum: Egrediamur foras. (Gen.4:8)
   And Cain said towards Abel his brother: let us go out outside.

2. Nec loqueris contra proximum tuum falsum testimonium. (Dt.5:20)
   Neither shall you speak false testimony against your neighbor.

3. Dominum Deum vestrum sequimini, et ipsum timete, et mandata illius custodite, et audite vocem ejus. (Dt.13:4)
   Follow the Lord our God, and fear the same, and guard his commands, and listen to his voice.

4. Benedicat tibi Dominus, et custodiat te. Ostendat Dominus faciem suam tibi, et misereatur tui. (Num.6:24-25)
   May the Lord bless you and guard you. May the Lord show his face to you and have mercy on you.

5. Laetetur mons Sion, et exsultent filiae Judae, propter judicia tua, Domine. (Ps.47:12)
   Let Mount Zion rejoice, and let the daughters of Judah exult, on account of your judgments, O Lord.

6. Confitebor tibi, Domine, in toto corde meo. (Ps.110:1)
   I give thanks to you, Lord, in all my heart.

7. Propter fratres meos et proximos meos loquebar pacem de te. (Ps.121:8)
   On account of my brothers and my neighbors I was speaking peace about you.

8. Confitemini Domino quoniam bonus, quoniam in aeternum misericordia ejus. Confitemini Deo deorum, quoniam in aeternum misericordia ejus. Confitemini Domino dominorum, quoniam in aeternum misericordia ejus. (Ps.135:1-3)
   Give thanks to the Lord because he is good, because his mercy is into eternity. Give thanks to the God of gods, because his mercy is into eternity. Give thanks to the Lord of lords, because his mercy is into eternity.

9. Dulcis est somnus operanti. (Ecc.5:12)
   Sleep is sweet to the one working.

10. Viventes enim sciunt se esse morituros. (Ecc.9:5)
    For the living know themselves to be going to die.

11. Egredimini et videte, filiae Sion, regem Salomonem in diademate quo coronavit illum mater sua in die desponsationis illius, et in die laetitiae cordis ejus. (SS.3:11)
    Go out and see, daughters of Zion, King Solomon in the diadem with which his own mother has crowned him, in the day of his espousals, and in the day of the rejoicing of his heart.

12. Quae est ista quae progreditur quasi aurora consurgens, pulchra ut luna, electa ut sol, terribilis ut castrorum acies ordinata? (SS.6:9)
    Who is this who goes forth as if the rising dawn, beautiful as the moon, chosen as the sun, terrible as an army drawn up for battle?

13. Aperui os meum, et locutus sum. (Sir.51:33)
    I have opened my mouth, and I have spoken.

14. Antequam loquaris, disce. (Sir.18:19)
    Before you should speak, learn.

15. Lauda, filia Sion; jubila, Israel: laetare, et exsulta in omni corde, filia Jerusalem. (Zeph.3:14)
    Praise, O daughter Zion; jubilate, O Israel; rejoice and exult in all the heart, O daughter Jerusalem.

16. Dominus Deus tuus in medio tui fortis, ipse salvabit: gaudebit super te in laetitia, silebit in dilectione sua, exsultabit super te in laude. (Zeph.3:17)
    The Lord your God is in the midst of you, strong; the same will save. He will rejoice over you in rejoicing; he will be silent in his love, he will exult over you in praise.

17. Beati misericordes: quoniam ipsi misericordiam consequentur. (Mt.5:7)
    Blessed are the merciful, because the same will follow with (receive) mercy.

18. Beati qui persecutionem patiuntur propter justitiam: quoniam ipsorum est regnum caelorum. (Mt.5:10)
    Blessed are they who suffer persecution on account of justice, because of the same is the kingdom of the heavens.

19. Ex abundantia enim cordis os loquitur. (Mt.12:34)
    For out of the abundance of the heart the mouth speaks.

20. Ecce nos dimisimus omnia, et secuti sumus te. (Mk.10:28)
    Behold, we have sent away all things and have followed you.

21. Ego sum lux mundi; qui sequitur me, non ambulat in tenebris sed habebit lumen vitae. (Jn.8:12)
I am the light of the world; he who follows me does not walk in the shadows but will have the light of life.

22. Maria ergo, cum venisset ubi erat Jesus, videns eum, cecidit ad pedes ejus, et dicit ei: Domine, si fuisses hic, non esset mortuus frater meus. (Jn.11:32)
Therefore, Mary, when she had come where Jesus was, seeing him, fell towards his feet and says to him, "Lord, if you had been here, my brother would not have died."

23. Si quis mihi ministrat, me sequatur, et ubi sum ego, illic et minister meus erit. (Jn.12:26)
If [any]one ministers to me, he should follow me, and where I am, there also my minister will be.

24. Haec locutus sum vobis: ut gaudium meum in vobis sit, et gaudium vestrum impleatur. (Jn.15:11)
These things I have spoken to y'all, so that my joy may be in y'all, and your joy may be filled.

25. Haec locutus sum vobis, ut in me pacem habeatis. In mundo pressuram habebitis: sed confidite, ego vici mundum. (Jn.16:33)
These things I have spoken to y'all, so that y'all may have peace in me. In the world y'all will have pressure, but trust, I have conquered the world.

26. Omnis lingua confiteatur, quia Dominus Jesus Christus in gloria est Dei Patris. (Phil.2:11)
Let every tongue confess that the Lord Jesus Christ in glory is of God the Father.

27. Spera in Deo, quoniam adhuc confitebor illi: salutare vultus mei, et Deus meus. (at Mass, Ps.42:5)
Hope in God, because I will give thanks to him still: the salvation of my face and my God.

28. Et plebs tua laetabitur in te. (at Mass)
And your common people will rejoice in you.

29. Misereatur tui omnipotens Deus, et dimissis peccatis tuis, perducat te ad vitam aeternam. (at Mass)
May the almighty God have mercy on you and, with your sins having been sent away, lead you through towards eternal life.

30. Regina caeli, laetare, alleluia. Quia quem meruisti portare, alleluia, resurrexit, sicut dixit, alleluia. Gaude et laetare, Virgo Maria, alleluia, quia surrexit Dominus vere, alleluia. (Easter Antiphon)
    O Queen of heaven, rejoice, alleluia. Because he whom you merited to carry, alleluia, has risen, like he said, alleluia. Rejoice and rejoice, O Virgin Mary, alleluia, because the Lord has truly risen, alleluia.

31. Amore amoris tui, dicam tibi cum sancto Francisco, moriar, qui amore amoris mei dignatus es mori. (Alphonsus Liguori)
    With love of your love, I will say to you with Saint Francis: may I die, O you who have been worthy to die with the love of my love.

32. Loquere, Domine, quia audit servus tuus. O Jesu amantissime, tu venisti etiam hoc mane ad visitandam animam meam, ex intimo corde tibi gratias ago. (Alphonsus Liguori)
    Speak, Lord, because your servant listens. O most loving Jesus, you have come also this morning in order to visit my soul; I give thank to you out of the intimate heart.

33. O Jesu mi, tu mortuus es pro me, utinam ego etiam mori possem pro te et morte mea efficere, ut omnes ament te. (Alphonsus Liguori)
    O my Jesus, you died for me; would that I also be able to die for you and to make with my death so that all might love you.

34. Cor ad cor loquitur. (Augustine)
    Heart speaks to heart.

35. Roma locuta est; causa finita est. (Augustine)
    Rome has spoken, the cause has finished.

36. Moriamur igitur et ingrediamur in caliginem. (Bonaventure)
    Therefore, let us die and go in into the gloom.

37. Disce quasi semper victurus vive quasi cras moriturus. (Edmund of Abingdon)
    Learn as if always about to conquer, live as if tomorrow about to die.

38. Dilexi justitiam et odi iniquitatem; propterea morior in exilio. (the last words of Gregory VII)
    I have loved justice and I hate iniquity; therefore I die in exile.

39. Spiritus Sanctus etiam te ut habitaculum suum intuebatur. (Hildegard)
    The Holy Spirit also was gazing into you as his own little habitation.

40. Tu dedisti mihi verius cognoscere te, purius diligere te, sincerius credere in te, ardentius sequi te. (Hugo of St. Victor)
You have given to me to recognize you more truly, to love you more purely, to believe in you more sincerely, to follow you more ardently.

41. Unum agnosce, unum dilige, unum sequere, unum apprehende, unum posside. (Hugo of St. Victor)
Realize one, love one, follow one, apprehend one, possess one.

42. 'Audiam quid loquatur in me Dominus meus'. Beata anima quae Dominum in se loquentem audit. (a Kempis)
I will hear what my Lord might speak in me. Blessed is the soul which hears the Lord speaking in itself.

43. Domine Deus meus, tu es omnia bona mea. Et quis ego sum, ut audeam ad te loqui? Ego sum pauperrimus servulus tuus. (a Kempis)
O Lord my God, you are all my good things. And who am I that I should dare to speak towards you? I am your poorest little servant.

44. Omnis ratio et naturalis investigatio fidem sequi debet. (a Kempis)
Every reason and natural investigation ought to follow faith.

45. Moriendum enim certe est. (Cicero)
For going-to-die is certain.

46. Ante senectutem curavi ut bene viverem, in senectute ut bene moriar; bene autem mori est libenter mori. (Seneca)
Before old age I have cared so that I would live well, in old age so that I might die well, however to die well is to die freely.

47. Vincit qui patitur. (Persius)
He conquers who suffers.

48. In verbis tuis meditabor (episcopal motto)
In your words I will meditate.

49. Semper progrediens. (motto of Aruba)
Always going forward

50. Ex opere operato (theological term about the Sacraments)
Having worked out of the deed.

51. Ave, Imperator, morituri te salutant. (gladiatorial salute)
Hail, Emperor, those about to die greet you.

52. Tu vero, o mi Redemptor, quoniam pro me mortuus es, fac benigne ut amem te; te enim solum volo, nec extra te aliud quidpiam mihi opto. (Alphonsus Liguori, *Way of the Cross*)
Truly, you, O my Redeemer, because you died for me, make benignly that I might love you, for I want you alone, nor anything other outside you do I want to myself.

53. O sacrum Cor Jesu, salutis nostrae sitientissimum, revoca nos praevaricatores ad Cor, ut non moriamur in peccatis nostris. (*Little Office of the Sacred Heart of Jesus*)
O sacred Heart of Jesus, most thirsting of our salvation, call us apostates back towards the Heart so that we might not die in our sins.

54. O veritas, o caritas, o finis et felicitas, sperare fac et credere, amare fac et consequi. (*Aeterna Lux Divinitas*)
O truth, O charity, O end and happiness, make [me] to hope and to believe, make [me] to love and to follow.

55. Dies venit, dies tua, per quam reflorent omnia; laetemur in hac ut tuae per hanc reducti gratiae. (Ambrose, *Jam Christe Sol Justitiae*)
The day comes, your day, through which all things flower again; let us rejoice in this so that through this [we might] be having been led back to your grace.

56. Plagas, sicut Thomas, non intueor: Deum tamen meum te confiteor. Fac me tibi semper magis credere, in te spem habere, te diligere. (Aquinas, *Adoro Te Devote*)
I do not, like Thomas, look in your wounds: nevertheless, I confess you to be my God. Make me to believe you always more, to have hope in you, to love you.

57. Tantum ergo sacramentum veneremur. (Aquinas, *Pange Lingua*)
Therefore let us venerate so great a Sacrament.

58. Vitam praesta puram, iter para tutum, ut videntes Jesum, semper collaetemur. (*Ave Maris Stella*)
Bestow a pure life, prepare a safe journey, so that, seeing Jesus, we might always rejoice together.

59. Fac ut possim demonstrare, quam sit dulce te amare, tecum pati, tecum flere, tecum semper congaudere. (*De Amore Jesu*)
Make that I might be able to demonstrate how it should be to love you sweetly, to suffer with you, to weep with you, to always rejoice together with you.

60. Pro peccatis suae gentis, vidit Jesum in tormentis... vidit suum dulcem natum, morientem desolatum, dum emisit spiritum. (*Stabat Mater Dolorosa*)
For the sins of his own nation, she saw Jesus in torments. She saw her own sweet child, dying desolated, while he sent out the spirit.

61. O quam laeta et beata fuit illa immaculata, mater Unigeniti! (*Stabat Mater Speciosa*)
O how happy and blessed has been that immaculate Mother of the Only-begotten.

62. Quando corpus morietur, fac, ut animae donetur tui nati gloria. (*Stabat Mater Speciosa*)
When the body will die, make that the glory of your child should be given to the soul.

63. Domine Jesu, noverim me, noverim te, nec aliquid cupiam nisi te. Oderim me et amem te. Omnia agam propter te. Humiliem me, exaltem te. Nihil cogitem nisi te. Mortificem me et vivam in te. Quaecumque eveniant accipiam a te. Persequar me, sequar te, semperque optem sequi te. Fugiam me, confugiam ad te, ut merear defendi a te. Timeam mihi, timeam te, et sim inter electos a te... Aspice me, ut diligam te. Voca me, ut videam te, et in aeternum fruar te. (Augustine)
Lord Jesus, would that I have known myself, would that I have known you, nor that I should desire anything except you. Would that I might hate myself and love you. I will do all things because of you. May I humble myself, may I exalt you. May I think nothing except you. May I mortify myself and live in you. May I accept whatsoever should come out from you. May I follow through myself, may I follow you, and always may I wish to follow you. May I flee myself, may I flee towards you so that I might merit to be defended by you. May I fear to myself, may I fear you, and may I be among those chosen by you. Look at me that I might love you. Call me that I might see you and enjoy you into eternity.

64. Tota pulchra es, Maria. Et macula originalis non est in te. Tu gloria Jerusalem. Tu laetitia Israel. Tu honorificentia populi nostri. Tu advocata peccatorum. O Maria, O Maria. Virgo prudentissima. Mater clementissima. Ora pro nobis. Intercede pro nobis. Ad Dominum Jesum Christum. (Catholic Prayer)
You are all beautiful, Mary, and the original stain is not in you. You are the glory of Jerusalem. You are the rejoicing of Israel. You are the honor of our people. You are the advocate of sinners. O Mary, O Mary, virgin most prudent, mother most clement, pray for us, intercede for us towards the Lord Jesus Christ.

65. Dixit ei Jesus: Ego sum resurrectio et vita: qui credit in me, etiam si mortuus fuerit, vivet: et omnis qui vivit et credit in me, non morietur in aeternum. Credis hoc? Ait illi: Utique Domine, ego credidi quia tu es Christus, Filius Dei vivi, qui in hunc mundum venisti. (Jn.11:25-27)
Jesus said to him, "I am the resurrection and the life: he who believes in me, even if he should have been dead, will live, and everyone who lives and believes in me will not die into eternity. Do you believe this?" She says to him, "Yes, Lord, I have believed that you are Christ, the Son of the living God, who have come into this world."

66. Credo in Deum Patrem omnipotentem, Creatorem caeli et terrae. Et in Jesum Christum, Filium ejus unicum, Dominum nostrum, qui conceptus est de Spiritu Sancto, natus ex Maria Virgine, passus sub Pontio Pilato, crucifixus, mortuus, et sepultus, descendit ad inferos, tertia die resurrexit a mortuis, ascendit ad caelos, sedet ad dexteram Dei Patris omnipotentis, inde venturus est judicare vivos et mortuos. Credo in Spiritum Sanctum, sanctam Ecclesiam catholicam, sanctorum communionem, remissionem peccatorum, carnis resurrectionem, vitam aeternam. Amen. (Apostles' Creed)
    I believe in God the Father almighty, the Creator of heaven and earth, and in Jesus Christ his only Son, our Lord, who has been conceived about the Holy Spirit, born out of the Virgin Mary, suffered under Pontius Pilate, crucified, died, and buried. He descended towards hell. On the third day he rose from the dead, he ascended towards the heavens, he sits towards the right hand of God the Father almighty, from where he is going to come to judge the living and the dead. I believe in the Holy Spirit, the holy catholic Church, the communion of saints, the remission of sins, the resurrection of the flesh, and life eternal. Amen.

67. Credo in unum Deum, Patrem omnipotentem, factorem caeli et terrae, visibilium omnium et invisibilium. Et in unum Dominum Jesum Christum, Filium Dei unigenitum, et ex Patre natum ante omnia saecula. Deum de Deo, Lumen de Lumine, Deum verum de Deo vero, genitum non factum, consubstantialem Patri; per quem omnia facta sunt. Qui propter nos homines et propter nostram salutem descendit de caelis. Et incarnatus est de Spiritu Sancto ex Maria Virgine, et homo factus est. Crucifixus etiam pro nobis sub Pontio Pilato, passus et sepultus est, et resurrexit tertia die, secundum Scripturas, et ascendit in caelum, sedet ad dexteram Patris. Et iterum venturus est cum gloria, judicare vivos et mortuos, cujus regni non erit finis. Et in Spiritum Sanctum, Dominum et vivificantem, qui ex Patre Filioque procedit. Qui cum Patre et Filio simul adoratur et conglorificatur: qui locutus est per prophetas. Et unam, sanctam, catholicam et apostolicam Ecclesiam. Confiteor unum baptisma in remissionem peccatorum. Et expecto resurrectionem mortuorum, et vitam venturi saeculi. (Nicene Creed)
    I believe in one God, the Father almighty, maker of heaven and earth, of all things visible and invisible, and in one Lord Jesus Christ, the only-begotten Son of God, and born out of the Father before all ages: God down from God, light down from light, true God down from true God, begotten not made, consubstantial to the Father, through whom all things have been made, who on account of us humans and on account of our salvation descended down from the heavens. And he was incarnated about the Holy Spirit out of the virgin Mary and was made human. Also, he was crucified for us under Pontius Pilate, suffered, and was buried, and he rose again on the third day, according to the Scriptures, and he ascended into heaven. He sits towards the right hand of the Father. And he is going to come again with glory to judge the living and the dead, of whose kingdom there will not be an end. And in the Holy Spirit, the Lord and the one making life, who proceeds out of the Father and the Son, who at the same time is adored and glorified together with the Father and the Son, who spoke through the prophets. And one, holy, catholic, and Apostolic Church. I confess one baptism into the remission of sins, and I expect the resurrection of those having died, and the life of the age to come.

68. Te Deum laudamus: te Dominum confitemur. Te aeternum Patrem omnis terra veneratur. Tibi omnes Angeli, tibi caeli et universae potestates, tibi Cherubim et Seraphim incessabili voce proclamant: Sanctus, Sanctus, Sanctus, Dominus Deus Sabaoth. Pleni sunt caeli et terra majestatis gloriae tuae. Te gloriosus Apostolorum chorus, te Prophetarum laudabilis numerus, te Martyrum candidatus laudat exercitus. Te per orbem terrarum sancta confitetur Ecclesia: Patrem immensae majestatis, Venerandum tuum verum et unicum Filium, sanctum quoque Paraclitum Spiritum. Tu Rex gloriae, Christe. Tu Patris sempiternus es Filius. Tu ad liberandum suscepturus hominem, non horruisti Virginis uterum. Tu, devicto mortis aculeo, aperuisti credentibus regna caelorum. Tu ad dexteram Dei sedes, in gloria Patris. Judex crederis esse venturus. Te ergo quaesumus, tuis famulis subveni, quos pretioso sanguine redemisti. Aeterna fac cum sanctis tuis in gloria numerari. (Te Deum)
We praise you, God, we confess you (to be) Lord. All the earth venerates you eternal Father. To you all the angels, to you the heavens and all powers, to you Cherubim and Seraphim proclaim with unceasing voice: Holy, holy, holy Lord God of Hosts. Full are the heavens and the earth of the majesty of your glory. A glorious chorus of Apostles, a laudable number of prophets, a white-robed army of martyrs praise you. Holy Church through the globe of the lands confesses you: Father of immense majesty, your true and only Son to be venerated, also the Holy Spirit the Paraclete. You are the king of glory, O Christ. You are the everlasting Son of the Father. You, going to support human in order to liberate [him], were not horrified at the uterus of the virgin. You, with the sting of death conquered, opened the kingdoms of the heavens to those believing. You sit towards the right hand of God in the glory of the Father. You are believed to be about to come (as) Judge. Therefore we seek you: assist your servants whom you have redeemed with precious blood. Make [us] to be numbered with your saints in eternal glory.

Chapter Thirty-one

1. Peccator videbit, et irascetur... desiderium peccatorum peribit. (Ps.111:10)
   The sinner will see and will be angry... the desire of the sinners will perish.

2. Mitte panem tuum super transeuntes aquas, quia post tempora multa invenies illum. (Ecc.11:1)
   Send your bread over the waters going across, because after many times you will find it.

3. Et audivi vocem Domini dicentis: Quem mittam? et quis ibit nobis? Et dixi: Ecce ego, mitte me. (Isa.6:8)
   And I heard the voice of the saying Lord, "Whom shall I send? And who will go to (for) us?" And I said, "Behold, I! Send me."

4. Post haec autem designavit Dominus et alios septuaginta duos: et misit illos binos ante faciem suam in omnem civitatem et locum quo erat ipse venturus. (Lk.10:1)
However after these things the Lord designated also seventy-two others and sent them in pairs before his face into every city and place were he himself was about to come.

5. Respondit Jesus: Amen, amen dico tibi, nisi quis renatus fuerit ex aqua, et Spiritu Sancto, non potest introire in regnum Dei. (Jn.3:5)
Jesus responded, "Amen, amen I say to you, unless who should have been born again out of water and the Holy Spirit, he is not able to enter into the kingdom of God."

6. Sic enim Deus dilexit mundum, ut Filium suum unigenitum daret: ut omnis qui credit in eum non pereat sed habeat vitam aeternam. (Jn.3:16)
For thus has God loved the world, that he would give his only-begotten Son that everyone who believes in him might not perish but might have eternal life.

7. Dixit ergo Jesus ad duodecim: Numquid et vos vultis abire? Respondit ergo ei Simon Petrus: Domine, ad quem ibimus? Verba vitae aeternae habes: et nos credidimus, et cognovimus quia tu es Christus Filius Dei. (Jn.6:68-70)
Therefore Jesus said towards the twelve, "Surely y'all do not also want to go away?" Simon Peter responded therefore to him, "Lord, towards whom shall we go? You have the words of eternal life, and we have believed and have recognized that you are the Christ, the Son of God."

8. Sciens Jesus quia venit hora ejus ut transeat ex hoc mundo ad Patrem: cum dilexisset suos, qui erant in mundo, in finem dilexit eos. (Jn.13:1)
Jesus, knowing that his hour has come in order to that he might go across out of this world towards the Father: when he had loved his own who were in the world, he loved them into the end.

9. Sciens quia omnia dedit ei Pater in manus, et quia a Deo exivit, et ad Deum vadit… (Jn.13:3)
Knowing that the Father has given all things to him into hands, and that he went out from God and goes towards God...

10. Cum ergo exisset, dixit Jesus: Nunc clarificatus est Filius hominis, et Deus clarificatus est in eo. Si Deus clarificatus est in eo, et Deus clarificabit eum in semetipso: et continuo clarificabit eum. (Jn.13:31-32)
When therefore he had gone out, Jesus said, "Now is the Son of a human made renowned, and God is made renowned in him. If God is made renowned in him, God will also make him renowned him in himself, and he will make him renowned at once."

11. Et vidi caelum novum et terram novam. Primum enim caelum, et prima terra abiit, et mare jam non est. (Rev.21:1)
    And I saw a new heaven and a new earth. For the first heaven and the first earth has gone away, and the sea now is not.

12. Et introibo ad altare Dei: ad Deum qui laetificat juventutem meam. (at Mass, Ps.42:4)
    And I will go in towards the altar of God, towards God who makes joyful my youth.

13. Ite, missa est. (at Mass)
    Go, she has been sent.

14. O Sapientia, quae ex ore Altissimi prodiisti, attingens a fine usque ad finem, fortiter suaviterque disponens omnia: veni ad docendum nos viam prudentiae. (Advent Antiphon)
    O wisdom, you who have gone forward out of the mouth of the Most High, touching towards from end all the way towards end, strongly and sweetly arranging all things: come in order to teach us the way of prudence.

15. Parce Domine, parce populo tuo: ne in aeternum irascaris nobis. (Lent Antiphon; see Jl.2:17)
    Spare, O Lord, spare your people: may you not be angry to us into eternity.

16. Homines transeunt. (a Kempis)
    Humans go across.

17. O quam cito transit gloria mundi! (a Kempis)
    O how quickly the glory of the world goes across!

18. Pereant qui ante nos nostra dixerunt. (Aelius Donatus)
    May they perish who have said our things before us.

19. Loqui ignorabit qui tacere nesciet. (Ausonius)
    He will be ignorant to speak who will not know to refrain from speaking.

20. Vox audita perit. (Horace)
    A voice having been heard perishes.

21. Medio tutissimus ibis. (Ovid)
    You will go safest with the middle.

22. Tarde sed graviter vir sapiens irascitur. (Publilius Syrus)
    A wise man is angry slowly but seriously.

23. Potest ex casa magnus vir exire. (Seneca)
    A great man is able to go out out of a small house.

24. Quae fuit durum pati, meminisse dulce est. (Seneca)
    What was hard to suffer is sweet to remember.

25. Veritas numquam perit. (Seneca)
    Truth never perishes.

26. Graviora manent. (Virgil)
    More serious things remain.

27. Euntes docete omnes gentes (episcopal motto)
    Going, teach all nations.

28. Euntes evangelium praedicate (episcopal motto)
    Going, proclaim the Gospel.

29. Surgite eamus (episcopal motto)
    Rise, let us go.

30. Fiat justitia et pereat mundus. (motto of Ferdinand I of the Holy Roman Empire)
    Let justice happen and the world perish.

31. Ite ad Joseph. (Catholic phrase)
    Go towards Joseph.

32. Deridens alium, non inderisus abibit. (Latin Proverb)
    The one deriding another will not go away underided.

33. Quod cito fit, cito perit. (Latin Proverb)
    That which happens quickly, quickly perishes.

34. Pie Pelicane, Jesu Domine, me immundum munda tuo sanguine: cujus una stilla salvum facere totum mundum quit ab omni scelere. (Aquinas, *Adoro Te Devote*)
    O pious pelican, Lord Jesus, clean unclean me with your blood, whose one drop is able to make saved all the world from every crime.

35. Verbum, quod ante saecula e mente Patris prodiit, e Matris alvo Virginis, mortalis Infans nascitur. (Augustine Thomas Ricchini, *Caelestis Aulae Nuntius*)
    The Word which went forth before the ages out of the mind of the Father, out of the womb of the Virgin Mother, is born a mortal infant.

36. O Deus ego amo te, nec amo te ut salves me, nec quod qui te non diligunt aeterno igne pereunt. (*O Deus Ego Amo Te*)
O God I love you, nor do I love you so that you might save me, nor because they who do not love you perish with eternal fire.

37. Ne irascaris Domine, ne ultra memineris iniquitatis: ecce civitas Sancti facta est deserta: Sion deserta facta est: Jerusalem desolata est: domus sanctificationis tuae et gloriae tuae, ubi laudaverunt te patres nostri. (*Rorate Caeli*)
May you not be angry, Lord, may you not remember further of iniquity: behold, the city of the Holy One has been made a desert. Zion has been made a desert; Jerusalem is desolated, the house of your sanctification and your glory where our fathers praised you.

38. Vexilla regis prodeunt: fulget crucis mysterium, quo carne carnis conditor, suspensus est patibulo. (Venantius Fortunatus, *Vexilla Regis*)
The banners of the king go forward, the mystery of the Cross glistens on which the builder of flesh with flesh has been suspended with a gibbet.

39. Paulus Apostolus Jesu Christi per voluntatem Dei, et Timotheus frater: eis, qui sunt Colossis, sanctis, et fidelibus fratribus in Christo Jesu. Gratia vobis, et pax a Deo Patre nostro, et Domino Jesu Christo. Gratias agimus Deo, et Patri Domini nostri Jesu Christi semper pro vobis orantes: audientes fidem vestram in Christo Jesu, et dilectionem quam habetis in sanctos omnes propter spem. (Col.1:1-5)
Paul, an Apostle of Jesus Christ through the will of God, and Timothy the brother: to those who are at Colossae, to the saints, and to the faithful brothers in Christ Jesus. Grace to y'all and peace from God our Father and the Lord Jesus Christ. We give thanks to God and Father of our Lord Jesus Christ always praying for y'all, hearing (of) your faith in Christ Jesus and the love which y'all have in all the saints because of hope.

40. Oremus. Deus, qui nobis sub Sacramento mirabili Passionis tuae memoriam reliquisti; tribue, quaesumus, ita nos Corporis et Sanguinis tui sacra mysteria venerari, ut redemptionis tuae fructum in nobis jugiter sentiamus: qui vivis et regnas in saecula saeculorum. Amen. (Benediction)
Let us pray. O God, who have relinquished to us a memory of your Passion under marvelous Sacrament, grant, we seek, us so to venerate the sacred mysteries of your Body and Blood so that we might sense the fruit of your redemption in us perpetually, you who live and reign into the ages of ages. Amen.

Chapter Thirty-two

1. A solis ortu usque ad occasum laudabile nomen Domini. (Ps.112:3)
From the rising all the way towards the setting of the sun, the name of the Lord is laudable.

2. Utilior est sapientia cum divitiis, et magis prodest videntibus solem. (Ecc.7:12)
   Wisdom is more useful with riches, and it is more beneficial to those seeing the sun.

3. Beati qui lugent: quoniam ipsi consolabuntur. (Mt.5:5)
   Blessed are they who lament, because the same will be consoled.

4. Et dicebat: Qui habet aures audiendi, audiat. (Mk.4:9)
   And he was saying, "He who has ears of earing, let him hear."

5. O Radix Jesse, qui stas in signum populorum, super quem continebunt reges os suum, quem Gentes deprecabuntur: veni ad liberandum nos, jam noli tardare. (Advent Antiphon)
   O root of Jesse, you who stand into (as) a sign of the peoples, over whom kings will restrain their mouth, whom the nations will pray to: come in order to liberate us, now do not be late.

6. Inquirendo veritatem percipimus. (Abelard)
   We perceive the truth with inquiring.

7. O Maria, Mater Dei, et mater mea, tu etiam deprecare Jesum pro me. (Alphonsus Liguori)
   O Mary, Mother of God, and my mother, you also pray to Jesus for me.

8. Festinamus ad Christum non currendo sed credendo. (Augustine)
   We hurry towards Christ not with running but with believing.

9. Non dubia sed certa conscientia, Domine, amo te. Percussisti cor meum verbo tuo, et amavi te. (Augustine)
   With a certain not doubtful conscience, O Lord, do I love you. You have pierced my heart with your word, and I have loved you.

10. O Domine Jesu, adoro te a morte resurgentem et in caelum ascendentem, sedentemque ad dexteram Patris. Deprecor te, ut illuc te sequi et tibi praesentari merear. (Gregory the Great)
    O Lord Jesus, I adore you rising from death and ascending into heaven and sitting towards the right hand of the Father. I beseech you that thither I might merit to follow you and to be presented to you.

11. O Domine Jesu, adoro te in Cruce pendentem, coronam spineam in capite portantem. Deprecor te, ut tua Crux liberet me ab Angelo percutiente. (Gregory the Great)
    O Lord Jesus, I adore you hanging on the Cross, carrying a thorny crown on the head. I beseech you that your Cross might liberate me from the piercing angel.

12. O felix anima cujus corpus de terra ortum est. (Hildegard)
    O happy soul whose body has risen from the earth.

13. Sed scio, et veraciter ex toto corde meo credo, et ore confiteor, qui tu potes me facere dignum. (Jean de Fecamp)
    But I know, and truthfully out of all my heart I believe, and [out of] my mouth I confess you who are able to make me worthy.

14. Ausi sumus uti in hoc loco Danielis exemplo, non ignorantes, quoniam in hebraeo positum non est, sed quoniam in Ecclesiis tenetur. (Jerome)
    We have dared to use in this place the example of Daniel, not being ignorant that it is not having been put in Hebrew but that it is held in the churches.

15. Qui sequitur me non ambulat in tenebris dicit Dominus. Haec sunt verba Christi, quibus admonemur quatenus vitam ejus et mores imitemur, si volumus veraciter illuminari, et ab omni caecitate cordis liberari. Summum igitur studium nostrum, sit in vita Jesu meditari. (a Kempis)
    He who follows me does not walk in shadows, says the Lord. These are the words of Christ, with which we are admonished how far his life and customs we should imitate, if we want truly to be illuminated and to be liberated from every blindness of heart.

16. Precor te custos meus ut si fieri possit notum mihi facias finem meum. Et, cum de hoc corpore ductus fuero, non dimittas malignos spiritus terrere me. (Nicolas Salicetus)
    I pray to you, my guardian, so that, if it should be able to happen, you might make my end known to me. And, when I will have been led down from this body, you might not send away malignant spirits to terrify me.

17. Difficile est dictu, Quirites, quanto in odio simus. (Cicero)
    It is difficult to say, Quirites, how much we might be in hatred.

18. Quaerunt quid optimum factu sit. (Cicero)
    They seek what might be best to do.

19. Natura beatis, omnibus esse dedit, si quis cognoverit uti. (Claudian)
    Nature has given to all to be blessed, if [any]one should have recognized to use [it].

20. Nihil dignum dictu (Livy)
    Nothing is worthy to say.

21. Miserabile visu (Ovid)
    Miserable to see

22. Spectatum veniunt. (Ovid)
    They come to watch.

23. Nil est dictu facilius. (Terence)
    Nothing is more doable to say.

24. Mirabile dictu (Virgil)
    Marvelous to say

25. In serviendo consumor (episcopal motto)
    I am consumed in serving.

26. Et cetera (commonly abbreviated as *etc.*)
    And the rest

27. Precamur sancte Domine, hac nocte nos custodias; sit nobis in te requies, quietas horas tribue. (*Christe qui Splendor et Dies*)
    We pray, O holy Lord, you might guard us this night, let rest be to us in you, grant quiet hours.

28. Te mane laudum carmine, te deprecamur vespere. (*Jam Sol Recedit Igneus*)
    We beseech you with a song of praises in the morning, in the evening.

29. Eia mater fons amoris, me sentire vim doloris, fac ut tecum lugeam; fac ut ardeat cor meum, in amando Christum Deum, ut sibi complaceam. (*Stabat Mater Dolorosa*)
    O mother, fountain of love, make me to sense the strength of sorrow so that I might lament with you; make that my heart might burn in loving Christ God so that I might be pleasing with (you) to him.

30. Stabat mater dolorosa, juxta crucem lacrimosa, dum pendebat filius; cujus animam gementem, contristatam et dolentem, pertransivit gladius. (*Stabat Mater Dolorosa*)
    The sorrowful mother was standing next to the tearful Cross while the Son was hanging, whose groaning, saddened, and sorrowing soul a sword has gone across through.

31. Impleta sunt quae concinit, David fideli carmine, dicendo nationibus: regnavit a ligno Deus. (Venantius Fortunatus, *Vexilla Regis*)
    They are having been filled which David sings together with a faithful song, saying to the nations: God has reigned from wood.

32. Veni veni O Oriens! (*Veni Veni Emmanuel*)
    Come, come, O rising one!

33. Finem loquendi pariter omnes audiamus. Deum time, et mandata ejus observa: hoc est enim omnis homo, et cuncta quae fiunt adducet Deus in judicium pro omni errato, sive bonum, sive malum illud sit. (Ecc.12:13-14)
Let us all equally hear the end of speaking. Fear God, and observe his commands: for this is every human, and all things which happen God will lead towards into judgment for every error, whether that should be good or bad.

34. Te laudamus Domine omnipotens, qui sedes super Cherubim et Seraphim. Quem benedicunt Angeli, Archangeli; et laudant Prophetae et Apostoli. Te laudamus Domine orando, qui venisti peccata solvendo. Te deprecamur magnum Redemptorem, quem Pater misit ovium pastorem. Tu es Christus Dominus Salvator, qui de Maria Virgine es natus. *(Te Laudamus)*
We praise you, almighty Lord, you who sit over the Cherubim and Seraphim, whom the angels, archangels bless, and the prophets and apostles praise. We praise you, Lord, with praying, you who came with releasing sins. We pray to you, great Redeemer, whom the Father sent to be shepherd of the sheep. You are Christ, Lord, Savior, who about the Virgin Mary have been born.

35. Deus meus, ex toto corde paenitet me omnium meorum peccatorum, eaque detestor, quia peccando, non solum poenas a te juste statutas promeritus sum, sed praesertim quia offendi te, summum bonum, ac dignum qui super omnia diligaris. Ideo firmiter propono, adjuvante gratia tua, de cetero me non peccaturum peccandique occasiones proximas fugiturum. Amen. (Act of Contrition)
My God, out of all the heart I repent of all my sins, and I detest them, because with sinning, not only have I merited established punishments from you justly, but particularly because I have offended you, the highest good, and worthy, who should be loved over all things. Therefore, firmly I put forth about the rest, with your grace helping, myself to be not going to sin and to be going to flee the near occasions of sinning.

Chapter Thirty-three

1. Esto vir. (1Kgs.2:2)
   Be a man!

2. Veni, dilecte mi, egrediamur in agrum. (SS.7:11)
   Come, my beloved, let us go out into the field.

3. Beati mites: quoniam ipsi possidebunt terram. (Mt.5:4)
   Blessed are the meek, because the same will possess the earth.

4. Estote ergo vos perfecti sicut et Pater vester caelestis perfectus est. (Mt.5:48)
   Therefore, y'all be having been perfected as your heavenly Father also is having been perfected.

5. Si fueris Romae, Romano vivito more; si fueris alibi, vivito sicut ibi. (Ambrose)
   If you should have been at Rome, live with the Roman custom; if you should have been elsewhere, live as there.

6. Crescentem sequitur cura pecuniam. (Horace)
   Care follows growing money.

7. Militat omnis amans. (Ovid)
   Every loving person is a soldier.

8. Ut ameris, amabilis esto. (Ovid)
   In order that you might be loved, be lovable.

9. Nulla avaritia sine poena est. (Seneca)
   No greed is without punishment.

10. Gratior et pulchro veniens in corpore virtus. (Virgil)
    And virtue is more serious coming in a beautiful body.

11. Esto fidelis usque ad mortem (episcopal motto)
    Be faithful all the way towards death.

12. Esto mater propitia (episcopal motto)
    Be a favorable mother.

13. Esto vigilans (episcopal motto)
    Be one keeping vigil.

14. Esto vir fortis et labora sicut bonus miles Christi Jesu (episcopal motto)
    Be a strong man and work like a good soldier of Christ Jesus.

15. Estote factores verbi (episcopal motto)
    Be doers of the word.

16. Esto perpetua (motto of Idaho)
    Be perpetual.

17. Salus populi suprema lex esto (motto of Missouri)
    The salvation of the people, be the supreme law.

18. Esto laborator et erit Deus auxiliator. (Catholic phrase)
    Be a laborer and God will be a helper.

19. Veni, Redemptor gentium; ostende partum Virginis; miretur omne saeculum; talis decet partus Deum. (Ambrose, *Veni Redemptor Gentium*)
    Come, Redeemer of the nations; show the birth of the virgin; let every age marvel; thus a birth adorns God.

20. Solve vincla reis, profer lumen caecis, mala nostra pelle, bona cuncta posce. (*Ave Maris Stella*)
    Release the chains of the guilty, bring forth light to the blind, hurl out our bad things, request all good things.

21. Angelus fortis Gabriel! ut hostem pellat antiquum. (*Christe Sanctorum*)
    Strong angel Gabriel! Oh may he hurl out the ancient enemy.

22. Nox atra rerum contegit terrae colores omnium: nos confitentes poscimus te, juste judex cordium. (Gregory the Great, *Nox Atra Rerum*)
    A dark night covers the colors of all things of the earth: we, giving thanks, request you, just judge of hearts.

23. Hostem repellas longius pacemque dones. (Rabanus Maurus, *Veni Creator Spiritus*)
    May you repel the enemy farther, and may you grant peace.

24. Custodes hominum psallimus angelos, naturae fragili quos Pater addidit caelestis comites, insidiantibus ne succumberet hostibus. (Robert Bellarmine, *Custodes Hominum Psallimus*)
    We sing the guardians of humans, the angels, heavenly companions whom the Father has given to a fragile nature lest it might succumb to the ensnaring enemies.

25. Te lucis ante terminum, rerum creator poscimus, ut solita clementia, sis praesul ad custodiam. (*Te Lucis ante Terminum*)
    O Creator of things, we request you before the end of light that, with accustomed clemency, you might be a protector towards protection.

26. Ecce angelus Domini apparuit in somnis Joseph, dicens: Surge, et accipe Puerum et Matrem ejus, et fuge in Aegyptum, et esto ibi usque dum dicam tibi; futurum est enim, ut Herodes quaerat Puerum ad perdendum Eum. (Mt 2:13)
    Behold, the angel of the Lord appeared in sleeps to Joseph, saying, "Arise and receive the boy and his mother and flee into Egypt, and be there all the way while I will say to you; for it is about to be that Herod might seek the boy in order to destroy him.

27. Ave verum Corpus natum de Maria Virgine: vere passum, immolatum in cruce pro homine: cujus latus perforatum fluxit aqua et sanguine. Esto nobis praegustatum mortis in examine: O Jesu dulcis! O Jesu pie! O Jesu fili Mariae. (Innocent VI, *Ave Verum Corpus*)
Hail true Body born down from the Virgin Mary: truly having suffered, been sacrificed on the Cross for human: whose side having been pierced flowed with water and blood. Be a foretaste to us in the examination of death: O sweet Jesus! O pious Jesus! O Jesus son of Mary!

28. Credo quod sis angelus sanctus, a Deo omnipotente ad custodiam mei deputatus. Propterea peto et, per illum qui te ad hoc ordinavit, humiliter imploro ut me miseram fragilem atque indignam semper et ubique in hac vita custodias, protegas a malis omnibus atque defendas, et cum Deus hinc animam meam migrare jusserit, nullam in eam potestatem daemonibus habere permittas, sed tu eam leniter a corpore suscipias, et in sinu Habrae suaviter usque perducas jubente ac juvante creatore ac salvatore Deo nostro, qui est benedictus in saecula saeculorum. Amen. (Aelfwine)
I believe that you may be a holy angel, having been considered down from almighty God towards the protection of me. Therefore, I seek and, through that one who ordained you towards this, I implore humbly that you might guard miserable and fragile and unworthy me always and everywhere in this life, [that] you might protect and defend [me] from all bad things, and, when God shall have ordered my soul to migrate from here, may you permit to the demons to have no power in it, but may you gently receive it from the body, and in the bosom of Abraham sweetly may you lead [it] through all the way, with God our Creator and Savior ordering and helping, who is blessed into the ages of ages. Amen.

Printed in Great Britain
by Amazon